CONTENTS

W9-DIW-207

Success in Writing

Grammar Skills for Writers

GLOBE FEARON
Pearson Learning Group

Reviewers

Susan Dunlap
Program Assistant, Bilingual/ELD Services
West Contra Costa Unified School District
Richmond, CA

Elizabeth A. Hanson
English and Latin Teacher
Sheridan Middle School–High School
Thornville, OH

Norma J. Whittaker
Teacher, Dallas Public Schools
Pearl C. Anderson Middle Learning Center
Dallas, TX

Director of Editorial and Marketing, Secondary Supplementary: Nancy Surridge
Executive Editor: Jean Liccione
Project Editor: Lynn W. Kloss
Editor: Brian Hawkes
Editorial Assistant: Ryan Jones
Writer: Sandra Widener
Production Editor: Alan Dalgleish
Market Manager: Rhonda Anderson
Managing Editor: Leslee Terpay
Art Director: Josée Ungaretta
Electronic Page Production: Flanagan's Publishing Services, Inc.
Interior Design: Lisa Nuland
Cover Design: Leslie Baker

ISBN 0-835-92271-5
Printed in the United Stated of America

8 9 10 11 12 13 14 15   05 04 03

1-800-321-3106
www.pearsonlearning.com

UNIT 1 Understanding Sentences

You use sentences daily in speaking and writing. *I like chocolate ice cream. When are we going to the movies? Dance with me. That's a great T-shirt!* These are all sentences.

Define It

A **sentence** is a unit of thought. It can tell you something, ask you something, order you to do something, or express strong feelings.

Understand It

▶ How much do you already know about sentences? Read the following paragraphs. The first is correct, while the second has errors.

Example A
Have you ever seen a giant panda? Although some people call it a panda bear, it is not really a bear. Instead, pandas are related to raccoons. Because they mainly eat bamboo, pandas are found only in areas where there is enough bamboo to eat, such as in China and Tibet.

Example B
Have you ever seen a giant panda. Although some people call it a panda bear. It is not really a bear. Pandas are related to raccoons. Because they mainly eat bamboo. Pandas are found only in areas where there is enough bamboo to eat. Such as in China and Tibet.

Apply It

1. Use what you know about sentences to discuss Example A with a classmate. Decide why you think each sentence is correct.

2. Now discuss Example B. Which sentences are incorrect? How would you correct these sentences?

3. Fill out the first two columns in the chart below with what you know and what you want to know about sentences. At the end of the unit, fill out the third column.

What I Know	What I Want to Know	What I Learned

CHAPTER 1   Identifying the Purposes of Sentences

Why do sentences have different purposes? We need the different kinds of sentences to be able to say what we want to say—from asking questions to making demands.

Define It

In this chapter, you will learn how to identify sentences by their purpose. Each of the four kinds of sentences has a different purpose.

Understand It

▶ On the lines below, try writing sentences with different purposes.

1. Write a sentence that tells someone something.

_____

_____

2. Write a sentence that asks a question.

_____

_____

3. Write a sentence that commands someone to do something.

_____

_____

4. Write a sentence that shows a strong feeling you have.

_____

_____

Apply It

5. In small groups, discuss the following sentences. What are the differences between these sentences? When would you use each type of sentence?

We will mail the letter on time.
Did you mail the letter on time?
Mail the letter on time.
We mailed it on time!

Lesson 1   Declarative Sentences

Let's begin at the beginning. A **sentence** is a group of words that expresses a complete thought. *The cereal in the bowl* is not a complete thought. But read this: *The cereal in the bowl is soggy.* That sentence does express a complete thought. It is also an example of the most common kind of sentence: the declarative sentence.

Define It

A **declarative sentence** makes a statement. Making a statement is the first purpose of sentences. Here are some examples of declarative sentences.

> Yesterday, I put cinnamon in my milk.
>
> Manuel has a tryout with the Yankees.
>
> My leg hurt after I fell off the chair.

TIP **More About Declarative Sentences** Declarative sentences always end with a period.

Understand It

How do you tell the difference between declarative sentences and other kinds of sentences? If a sentence is simply telling you something, it's a declarative sentence.

1. In the following passage, underline the declarative sentences.

> Hello, Sam? Are you watching the hurricane sweep down the coast on the TV news? It's amazing! Chickens are soaring through the air. The roofs of houses are flying down the streets. Now the announcer is talking. Did you hear that? That's right. It's headed straight for us!

2. How are the declarative sentences different from the other kinds of sentences in this paragraph?

_____

Apply It

3. On a separate sheet of paper, write a description of a family member. Use only declarative sentences.

Lesson 2 Interrogative Sentences

To *interrogate* means "to question." You may have heard this word used in a movie: "Jenkins, interrogate the prisoner. Find out what he knows." By now, you can probably guess what an interrogative sentence does.

Define It

An **interrogative sentence** asks a question. Asking a question is the second purpose of sentences. Here are some examples of interrogative sentences.

> Have you found the basketball you lost?
>
> Why are your shoes on the wrong feet?

 TIP **More About Interrogative Sentences** Interrogative sentences end with a question mark.

Understand It

▶ The sentences below are declarative sentences. Rewrite them as interrogative sentences. Here's an example.

> Ginny went to New York last month.
>
> Did Ginny go to New York last month?

1. Leann put her diamond necklace on the dresser.

_____

2. Tomorrow is the first day of spring.

_____

3. That book has a surprise ending.

_____

Apply It

4. Imagine you are going to interview someone famous. Write the name of the person here.

_____

5. On a separate sheet of paper, write five interrogative sentences you would use to find out what you want to know about the person.

Lesson 3   Imperative Sentences

Imperative sentences demand action: *Clean your room. Finish that homework before you do anything else. Pass me that chocolate cream pie.*

Define It

An **imperative sentence** makes a request or gives a command. Making a request is the third purpose of sentences. Here are some examples of imperative sentences.

> Pretend you don't see the chocolate on his face.
>
> Jeremy, remember to hold your breath when you're under water!
>
> Stop!

In imperative sentences, the subject is often not stated. When it's not stated, the subject is understood to be *you*. For example, in the sentence *Stop!*, the command is given to you, the person who is hearing or reading the sentence.

 More About Imperative Sentences Strong commands end with an exclamation point: *Stop that!* Mild commands end with a period: *Please sit down.*

Understand It

▶ Read these sentences and rewrite them as imperative sentences.

1. Would you please stop making that noise?

_____

2. Tanisha should stop watching so much TV.

_____

3. Would you like to win the tournament?

_____

Apply It

▶ Imperative sentences are often used to give directions. Imagine you are telling someone how to do something, such as dribble a basketball or find a movie theater.

4. On another sheet of paper, write a series of imperative sentences that gives directions for completing the activity.

Lesson 4   Exclamatory Sentences

You know exclamatory sentences when you hear them. Exclamatory sentences show urgency: *I can't hold on! We'll lose the game if you don't get a hit!* Be careful with exclamatory sentences, though. If you use too many of them, they lose their excitement.

Define It

An **exclamatory sentence** expresses strong feeling or emotion. Expressing strong feelings is the fourth purpose of sentences. Here are some examples of exclamatory sentences.

> That tiger is leaping toward your head!
>
> I never want to see you again!

 More About Exclamatory Sentences Exclamatory sentences end with an exclamation point. *Watch out for them!*

Understand It

If you're writing a story in which the hero is about to walk unknowingly into a burning building, you could have a character say, "There's a fire, Jack." You could also write, "There's a fire, Jack!" The second sentence shows urgency. It demonstrates that Jack is in real danger.

▶ Decide if these sentences should be exclamatory. At the end of each one, write the appropriate punctuation and your reason for your choice.

1. You're swerving into his lane _____

2. The concert's sold out _____

3. You make me furious _____

Apply It

4. Here's the beginning of a story. Finish it on another sheet of paper, using exclamatory sentences when appropriate.

> The light from the glowing box in the sky almost blinded Enrique and Marie. "What **is** that?" Marie asked.
>
> "I don't know, but we'd better hide!" Enrique said, as they dove behind a rock. At that moment, the beam of light passed over the rock and then returned.
>
> "Do you smell that?" Marie whispered in panic, as the rock began to melt. Soon the rock would be burned through!

1. Read the following paragraphs. They contain examples of the four purposes of sentences, but their punctuation is missing. Write the correct punctuation on the line that follows each sentence. Then label each sentence as follows: (*D*) for declarative, (*In*) for interrogative, (*Im*) for imperative, or (*E*) for exclamatory. The first sentence is done for you.

The coldest winter any of them remembered was the winter of the frozen words **.** __D__ Do you remember it ___ That was the winter up in Paul Bunyon's logging camp that was so cold the words froze right out of people's mouths ___ Right there on the ground, jumbled words and sentences piled up ___ It was amazing ___

Then, come spring, those words began to thaw ___ All over the county, people heard things they'd said last winter and cringed ___ Can you imagine the trouble it caused all over ___

Finally, Paul Bunyon put a stop to it ___ "Go inside until all the words have melted ___" That's what he told them ___ That may have saved the town ___

2. On a separate piece of paper, write a paragraph about something that happened in your life that surprised or scared you. You can also make up a story, if you prefer. Make sure to include examples of all four purposes of sentences in your work. Label each sentence as follows: (*D*) for declarative, (*In*) for interrogative, (*Im*) for imperative, and (*E*) for exclamatory.

CHAPTER 2 Recognizing Sentence Structure

Sentences need to say something. They also need to hold a reader's attention. You can do both of these things by varying the types of sentences you write.

Define It

When you read, you'll notice that some sentences are short, while others are not. Some sentences contain one idea, while others contain many ideas. Varying the structure of the sentences you write is one way to make your writing sound smoother and more interesting.

Understand It

1. Try rewriting this paragraph to combine some of the sentences. In this way, you'll add variety and interest to the paragraph.

> She tossed the anchor overboard. We had finally reached the island. We sang. We danced. We celebrated. The captain gave a speech. The first mate gave a speech. Only when we stopped celebrating did we notice one thing. We noticed the boat had drifted away from the island.

_____

_____

_____

_____

_____

_____

_____

_____

Apply It

2. Compare your paragraph with that of another classmate. Discuss why each of you made the changes you did and why the changes help make the paragraph sound more interesting.

Lesson 5   Subjects and Predicates

Did a terrific job. Who did a terrific job? You can't tell. Sentences need both a subject and a predicate to express a complete thought.

Define It

The **subject** is what or whom the sentence is about. Subjects can be nouns or pronouns. Nouns that can be subjects include *Matthew, the job,* and *the scientist.* Pronouns that can be subjects include *she, it,* and *they.*

The **simple subject** is the most important word in the complete subject. The **complete subject** may give more details about the simple subject. For example, in the sentence *The speckled cow stood in the field, cow* is the simple subject. *The speckled cow* is the complete subject.

The **predicate** is the verb or verb phrase that tells what the subject is doing. Verbs that can be predicates include *diving, will go,* and *is done.*

The **simple predicate** is just the verb itself. The **complete predicate** may give more details about the verb. For example, in the sentence *We should go to the beach, should go* is the simple predicate. *Should go to the beach* is the complete predicate.

 More About Subjects Even imperative sentences of one word, such as *Run!,* have a subject. As you learned in Lesson 3, the subject, *you,* is implied.

Understand It

A sentence has both a subject and a predicate. In this example, the subject is underlined once and the predicate is underlined twice.

> The yellow dog jumped over the moon. (**The yellow dog** is the complete subject; **dog** is the simple subject. **Jumped over the moon** is the complete predicate; **jumped** is the simple predicate.)

▶ Divide the following sentences into their complete subjects and predicates. Draw one line under each complete subject and two lines under each complete predicate. If a subject is implied, underline only the predicate.

1. Edward looked into the black cave gloomily.

2. No one saw the thief escape.

3. Dive off the high diving board into the pool.

Apply It

4. Find five or six sentences of writing you have done recently. Underline each complete subject once and each complete predicate twice.

Lesson 6   Simple Sentences

In the case of simple sentences, *simple* doesn't mean "short" or "easy to understand." Instead, it means that the sentence has a simple structure.

Define It

An **independent clause** is a group of words that has a subject and a predicate. It can stand alone as a **simple sentence**. Reading lots of short sentences, though, can be tiring. Compound subjects and predicates can help you create sentences that are more interesting to read.

Simple sentences may have compound subjects and predicates. **Compound subjects** have more than one simple subject. **Compound predicates** have more than one simple predicate. Here's a simple sentence with a compound subject and a compound predicate.

> Ben and Joan swam and danced. (**Ben and Joan** is the compound subject. **Swam and danced** is the compound predicate.)

Understand It

Simple sentences may be long or short. Here's a long simple sentence.

> You and that dog of yours can just let go of that steak. (**You and that dog of yours** is the complete subject. **Can just let go of that steak** is the complete predicate.)

More About Complete Sentences To test if a sentence is complete, underline the subject once and the predicate twice. If you have both and the sentence makes sense, it's complete.

Apply It

▶ Now try some sentence writing of your own.

1. Write a simple sentence with a simple subject and simple predicate.

_____

2. Write a simple sentence with a simple subject and a compound predicate.

_____

3. Write a simple sentence with a compound subject and a compound predicate.

_____

The bell chimed. We went in. These two sentences are correct. But by linking them, you can create a smoother sentence. *The bell chimed, and we went in.*

Define It

A **compound sentence** is made up of two or more independent clauses, any of which can stand alone as a simple sentence. You can join these simple sentences with a word such as *and*, *but*, or *or*. Here's an example.

> The tree fell. The house was not damaged.
>
> The tree fell, but the house was not damaged.

You can join independent clauses with a semicolon or with a semicolon and a word such as *also*, *however*, or *therefore*. Here are two examples.

> The tree fell; the house was not damaged.
>
> The tree fell; however, the house was not damaged.

To spot a compound sentence, look for a word such as *and* or *but*. You can also look for a semicolon. Then, look at each of the clauses. If each one makes sense on its own, you're reading a compound sentence.

Understand It

▶ Connect the following simple sentences to make compound sentences.

1. The calf whimpered. The wolves drew closer.

_____

2. The game was close. We finally won.

_____

Apply It

3. Rewrite the following paragraph on a separate sheet of paper so it contains some compound sentences. Try joining the sentences in different ways.

> In 1954, a businessman visited a restaurant. He liked what he saw. He bought that restaurant. He tried something different at his restaurant. He set up a new system. His workers could make hamburgers, milkshakes, and French fries very quickly, The idea caught on. He died in 1984. There were more than 750,000 restaurants in his chain.

Lesson 8   Complex Sentences

Complex sentences also make your writing flow. They help you show how your ideas relate to one another. For example, read this sentence: *When Fran lost her bracelet, she cried and cried.* The word *when* signals that Fran cried because she had lost her bracelet. It shows you the relationship between the ideas *Fran lost her bracelet* and *Fran cried and cried.*

Define It

A **complex sentence** has an independent clause and one or more dependent clauses. A **dependent clause** contains a subject and a predicate, but it cannot stand alone. The independent and dependent clauses in a complex sentence can be joined by words such as *because, where, unless,* and *whether.* The dependent clauses in the examples below are in **bold type**.

> **Until you swallow that bite,** you won't get another hot dog.
>
> **Whenever there's trouble,** Michael shows up **because he just can't stay away.**

 TIP **More About Complex Sentences** Words that can introduce dependent clauses include: *after, although, before, if, since, though, unless, until, when, whenever,* and *while.*

Understand It

Complex sentences can help you define the meaning of your sentences more precisely than compound sentences can. You can write *I waited until the chocolate cooled, and then I ate it.* That's a compound sentence. You can also write, *I waited until the chocolate cooled before I ate it.* The word *before* shows the order in which things happened.

1. Read the paragraph below and decide if each sentence is simple (*S*), compound (*CD*), or complex (*CX*). Write the symbol that describes each sentence above it.

> Jackie Robinson was a great baseball player. When people hear his name, though, they remember his great courage. Robinson was not only a great player; he was also the first African American to play in the major leagues. While fans booed, he kept his dignity. When pitchers threw at his head, he didn't flinch.

Apply It

2. On a separate sheet of paper, write a paragraph about someone you admire. Label each sentence simple (*S*), compound (*CD*), or complex (*CX*).

1. The following paragraphs of simple sentences could be made more interesting if the lengths of the sentences were varied. Use another sheet of paper to rewrite these paragraphs, combining some of the sentences into compound or complex sentences. Be sure to keep some of the sentences simple, too.

You've used paper cups. You've probably used them a thousand times. A man named Hugh Moore invented the paper cup. He didn't care about the cup, though. He had a different idea. He wanted to sell drinks of water.

In 1908, Hugh Moore built a vending machine. It was made of porcelain. He designed a paper cup. The paper cup would hold the water. Nobody bought the water, though. Later, Moore realized something. He could sell just the cups. That was a smashing success. Today, paper cups are a huge business.

2. Find a page of writing you have done. Rewrite it on another sheet of paper so that it uses the three kinds of sentences discussed in this chapter. Label each sentence as simple (*S*), compound (*CD*), or complex (*CX*).

CHAPTER 3   Constructing Sentences

Now you know how to write different types of sentences. Your next step is to learn how to make sure your reader gets your message.

Define It

When you write clearly, your reader understands what you want to say. Writing clearly means that words are where they belong and that a reader understands where a sentence is headed.

Understand It

▶ As you've learned in Chapters 1 and 2, sentences express a complete thought. They contain both a subject and a predicate. Look at the following sentences. Think about what's missing or confusing about each one. Then rewrite each sentence so it is complete and easy to understand.

1. Because they were our friends.

_____

2. We did our jobs, they helped us.

_____

3. They left the dog there they forgot about it.

_____

4. After looking down the street, the bicycle zoomed away.

_____

5. His friend borrowed a hammer wearing a toolbelt.

_____

Apply It

6. Compare your answers with a partner. What differences did you find in your revisions? Why do you think your revisions were different? How did your revisions change the meaning of the sentences?

Lesson 9   Phrases

You've probably heard the word *phrase*. You may have heard someone say, "Oh, I didn't mean it. It's just a phrase." In the study of writing, *phrase* has another meaning.

Define It

A **phrase** is a group of words that does not have a subject and a predicate and cannot stand alone. There are several types of phrases. All of these types are useful in sentences. Phrases are groups of words that act as a single part of speech. In these examples, the phrases are in **bold type**.

> **In the morning,** Janine must leave.
> **Covered with mud,** Marty emerged **from the swamp.**

More About Phrases There is one sure way to pick out phrases: They don't make sense alone. If a group of words has both a subject and predicate, it's a clause, not a phrase.

Understand It

Look again at the phrases in the examples above: *in the morning*, *covered with mud*, and *from the swamp*. None has both a subject and a predicate. Even though they cannot stand alone, phrases are necessary in writing. They explain, provide details, and give more information. The phrases in the examples above tell you the following information: when Janine must leave, where Marty was, and how he looked.

▶ In the sentences below, underline the phrases.

1. With all our packing done, we left for the airport.

2. We hoped to explore space.

3. Finding no chocolate, we ate licorice.

4. To be honest, we are leaving.

Apply It

5. Try doing some writing using different kinds of phrases. On another sheet of paper, write a paragraph about your favorite sport. Describe it and explain why it's your favorite. Underline the phrases you use.

Lesson 10　Misplaced Modifiers

Throw the cow over the fence some hay. Exactly what is going over the fence? Common sense tells you to throw the hay over the fence, but the sentence doesn't say this.

Define It

This is a case of a misplaced modifier. A **modifier** is a word or group of words that describes other words. A **misplaced modifier** is a modifier that is in the wrong position. For example, in the sentence *Happily, Lisa's tire was not ruined*, the word *happily* seems to modify *tire* instead of *Lisa*.

Misplaced modifiers can lead to confusion. Here is an example.

> *Unclear:* The seamstress held up the needle wearing the ruffled dress.
>
> *Clear:* The seamstress wearing the ruffled dress held up the needle.

More About Misplaced Modifiers Avoid constructions in which a modifier may refer to a word that is either before or after the modifier. For example, in the sentence *Dancing often excites her, often* could refer to *dancing*, or it could refer to *excites*. Rewrite the sentence as either *Often, dancing excites her,* or *It excites her to dance often.*

Understand It

When you use modifiers such as *almost, only, even, nearly, merely,* and *just,* avoid confusion by using them just before the words they modify. In the following example, the four sentences are exactly the same, except that the word *only* modifies different words. Notice the difference that moving this word makes.

> She only pretended to talk to them yesterday. (She was pretending, not really talking.)
>
> Only she pretended to talk to them yesterday. (She was the only person who was pretending.)
>
> She pretended to only talk to them yesterday. (She pretended to do nothing but talk.)
>
> She pretended to talk to them only yesterday. (She pretended at no other time.)

In general, the easiest way to keep misplaced modifiers from confusing your reader is to keep the modifier and what it is modifying as close as possible to one another. Doing so will make your meaning clear—and not unintentionally funny.

▶ Rewrite the following sentences so they are clear.

1. The lion jumped on the man with a growl.

_____

2. The state trooper said he had a few problems with a smile.

_____

3. The theater creates a good impression on visitors built 100 years ago.

_____

4. Carlo called for directions who is Anna's brother.

_____

Apply It

5. On the lines below, rewrite the following paragraphs so that their modifiers are all clearly attached to the words they should modify.

Alby stared at him in disbelief with a grin. "You can't mean she just let the ducks go?"

"Why, yes," Barney said who was watching the ducks. "She simply opened the cage quacking loudly, and out they went."

"From the north end I wanted to take pictures of them," Alby said. "Oh, well. They'll be famous anyway. Newspapers will carry the story of the ducks escaping all over the country."

_____

_____

_____

_____

_____

_____

_____

Lesson 11　Dangling Modifiers

Attached to nothing, floating in midair—that is the fate of dangling modifiers. Watch out for them. Like misplaced modifiers, dangling modifiers can confuse your reader.

Define It

A **dangling modifier** is a phrase, usually at the beginning of a sentence, that does not appear to be connected to anything in the sentence. By attaching the modifier to an incorrect word, usually the subject of the main clause, the writer creates confusion. Look at this example and its revision.

> *Unclear:* On leaving home, the door slammed shut. (Who left home?)
>
> *Clear:* The door slammed shut when Ellen left home.

More About Dangling Modifiers and Misplaced Modifiers
Misplaced modifiers seem to modify the wrong subject; dangling modifiers seem to have no subject of their own.

Understand It

▶ Rewrite the following sentences to clarify what the dangling modifier is modifying.

1. After reading the books all afternoon, the light finally dimmed.

_____

2. Rolling on the ground, the boy picked up the apple.

_____

3. Not being able to run a computer, a hacker walked over and helped me.

_____

Apply It

4. Rewrite this paragraph on another sheet of paper, eliminating the dangling modifiers.

> After waiting for hours, the snow began. Soft and fluffy, the children flung it into the air, squealing with happiness. Although only a small boy, my father expected me to stop playing and to shovel.

Lesson 12   Sentence Fragments

If a group of words looks like a sentence but doesn't make sense, check it. You may have a sentence fragment that is disguised as a sentence.

Define It

A **sentence fragment** is a phrase that lacks either a subject or a predicate. Dependent clauses may also be sentence fragments. Here are two examples.

> Like the friend you never had.
>
> Can help us find Chan's house.

More About Sentence Fragments Look for the subject and predicate of the sentence. If it has both, it's a complete sentence. (Remember that in imperative sentences, the subject—*you*—may not be stated.)

Understand It

You can deal with sentence fragments in two ways. You can add additional words to make them sentences, or you can join them to other sentences. For example, you might add *He acts* to the first example above to make the sentence read *He acts like the friend you never had.* You might also add *The road map* to the second example to make the sentence read *The road map can help us find Chan's house.*

▶ Rewrite these sentence fragments to make them sentences.

1. Because you told me to.

_____

2. My old house on the street with the cherry trees.

_____

3. My first dance. Whenever I think about it, I laugh.

_____

4. Thinking about the waste of time.

_____

Apply It

5. On another sheet of paper, write a description of your favorite piece of clothing. Read each sentence carefully to make sure you have not used any sentence fragments.

Lesson 13   Run-on Sentences

When you see a run-on sentence often you know it the sentence goes on forever. You probably wondered when that last sentence would end. You may even have lost track of what the sentence was about. Those are two signs of run-on sentences.

Define It

A **run-on sentence** strings together two or more sentences without using a linking word or punctuation to connect them. Here are two examples.

> Horror movies are awful they scare me.
>
> They were best friends they did everything together.

Understand It

You can easily fix run-on sentences in one of three ways. You can separate them into two or more sentences, you can add punctuation, or you can use a linking word such as *and*, *but*, or *or*. Here are examples of ways to fix the first run-on sentence above.

> Horror movies are awful. They scare me.
>
> Or: Horror movies are awful; they scare me.
>
> Or: Horror movies are awful, and they scare me.

1. On another sheet of paper, rewrite the following paragraph, eliminating the run-on sentences.

> Rob Roy was the Scottish Robin Hood he lived from 1671 to 1734 he was called Rob because it is the Scottish word for "red" and he had red hair. When he was 22 he became head of the MacGregor clan and inherited huge estates when they were taken from him he became an outlaw stealing cattle he was arrested and imprisoned in London. The famous book <u>Rob Roy</u> by Sir Walter Scott was based on his life Rob Roy's life was also the basis for a movie.

Apply It

2. Use another sheet of paper to write a paragraph about the last movie you saw and why you did or didn't like it. Read each sentence carefully to be sure that you have no run-on sentences in your work.

Lesson 14 Comma Faults

Commas can help a sentence make sense. They can also confuse readers by linking two sentences that don't belong together.

Define It

A **comma fault** occurs when a writer uses a comma alone to connect two sentences. Here's an example.

> Please fix dinner, remember I can't eat liver.

Understand It

You can fix a comma fault in four ways. You can use a word such as *and* or *but*, you can add a semicolon between the clauses, you can create two sentences, or you can change one of the clauses to a dependent clause. Here are examples of ways the comma fault above can be fixed.

> Please fix dinner, and remember I can't eat liver. (The word **and** makes this a compound sentence.)
>
> Please fix dinner; remember I can't eat liver. (The semicolon makes this a compound sentence.)
>
> Please fix dinner. Remember I can't eat liver. (The period divides one long sentence into two shorter sentences.)
>
> When you fix dinner, please remember I can't eat liver. (**When** makes the first part of this sentence a dependent clause.)

More About Finding Sentence Errors It's easiest to find fragments, run-on sentences, and comma faults when you revise. Read your sentences aloud or to yourself one at a time. Ask yourself if each sentence can stand alone and if each one clearly says what you want to say.

▶ On a separate sheet of paper, edit these sentences so that you fix the comma faults.

1. He played baseball, he played basketball.

2. One way is easy, the other way is hard.

3. She ran, there was no other way to escape.

Apply It

4. Write a paragraph about something you did today. Be sure that your writing *does* contain comma faults. Then switch papers with a classmate, and edit your classmate's paragraph so that it contains no comma faults.

Lesson 15   Wordiness and Rambling

One of the hardest things to do when you write is to keep your writing clear and concise. Here are some tips for doing that.

Define It

Wordiness weakens your writing. It is such a common problem, though, that entire books have been written on the subject. There are thousands of ways wordiness can creep into your writing. In the list below, see how many wordy phrases can be replaced by one word or two shorter words.

Wordy	Concise
at this point in time	now
during the time in question	then
due to the fact that	because
in the year of	in
during the same time that	while
was of the opinion that	believed
green in color	green
bitter-tasting medicine	bitter medicine
connect up together	connect
true facts	facts

■ Watch for redundancy, or saying something you've already said.

The pool is round **in shape**. (The phrase **in shape** adds nothing to the sentence because **round** is a kind of shape.)

■ Use pronouns to replace words.

Gerald saw the geese, and Gerald urged the geese to escape.

Better: Gerald saw the geese, and **he** urged **them** to escape.

■ Also, watch for rambling sentences.

> After I looked at some books, I read some more books about the subject.
>
> *Better*: I am reading many books about the subject.

Understand It

Weeding out wordiness and rambling takes a sharp eye. Examine every sentence you write to see where you can make its meaning clearer by replacing wordy phrasing.

▶ Rewrite these sentences to eliminate wordiness and rambling.

1. The car, which is red in color, is located in the lot behind the house.

_____

2. To a large extent, he did not offer much in the way of guidance.

_____

3. In the past, he said it, and then he said it again.

_____

4. In the event that he is ready in the very near future, we should go then.

_____

More About Wordiness Avoiding wordiness does not mean writing only short sentences. Compare *With a vicious snap, the dog angrily closed its powerful jaws* with *The dog closed its mouth*. Be sure your sentences include enough information so your reader can see the scene you're describing and follow your reasoning.

Apply It

5. On a separate sheet of paper, rewrite this paragraph to eliminate wordiness and rambling.

> Over the duration of the time we were in the sailboat, we began to realize that for our mutual survival, we had to cooperate together. The water was rising up into the boat more every minute. We also knew that although at 7:30 last night a boat came by our boat, we might not see another boat until many hours passed.

Lesson 16   Parallelism

The basketball players dribbled, passed, shot, and are rebounding well. Can you spot the error? It's the phrase *are rebounding well*—it's an error of parallelism. Parallelism creates a feeling of balance and rhythm. It also helps parts of sentences feel like they "belong" together.

Define It

Parallelism in writing is a form of repetition. It's a repetition of grammatical forms, as in the verbs *dribbled*, *passed*, and *shot*, in the example above. All of these verbs are in the past tense. The verb phrase *are rebounding* breaks that pattern because it's in the present tense. Here are some examples of parallelism.

Parallel nouns

Not parallel: She wanted to talk about baseball, sometimes football interested her, and hockey.

Parallel: She wanted to talk about baseball, football, and hockey. (The words **baseball**, **football**, and **hockey** are all nouns.)

Parallel phrases

Not parallel: He likes to eat popcorn, to watch movies, and rearranging the furniture.

Parallel: He likes to eat popcorn, watch movies, and rearrange the furniture.

Or: He likes eating popcorn, watching movies, and rearranging the furniture. (All of the verbs in both examples are in the same tense.)

Parallel clauses

Not parallel: When she painted the room, when she cleaned the windows, and because she washes the floor, her hands became sore.

Parallel: When she painted the room, when she cleaned the windows, and when she washed the floor, her hands became sore. (The clauses begin with **when** and the verbs are all in the same tense.)

You may need to repeat other elements in a sentence to make the forms parallel.

Not parallel: I could not do it, and had my reasons.

Parallel: I could not do it, and I had my reasons. (Both clauses have a subject and a verb.)

Understand It

▶ You can fix problems with parallelism by making sure that similar forms in a sentence use the same tense or structure. Change the following sentences so their forms are parallel.

1. Marge squirmed, lied, and try to pretend it never happened.

_____

2. Our tasks are to watch, to listen, and learning what we can.

_____

3. First Matt went to the dentist, then he went to the bakery, he goes to school.

_____

4. The software doesn't work, and disappointing everyone.

_____

Apply It

5. On the lines below, write a paragraph about what you do when you are getting ready to go to a movie. Use parallelism in at least three of the sentences you write.

_____

_____

_____

_____

_____

_____

1. The following paragraphs contain misplaced modifiers, dangling modifiers, comma faults, sentence fragments, wordiness, run-on sentences, and parallelism errors. On another sheet of paper, rewrite the paragraphs so these errors are eliminated.

Buying the right one, a bike can cost at least $200 in money shopping often makes it easier to choose the best bike for the money. If you spend that $200, for example. Here's what you can expect to buy. A sturdy frame. A wide seat. Multiple gears, and a shock-absorbing suspension. All of those features can help you make sure that you are certainly getting a bike that is comfortable, that rides well, and serving you for many years. A bike is a big purchase, you should shop wisely.

These hints make it clear why it is good to buy a bike from a buying guide. The buying guide, which will tell you how to buy. According to the buying guide, you should use these hints: know the kind of bike you want, decided on the key features important to you, and keep your price range in mind as you shop for a bike.

2. On another sheet of paper, write hints for shopping for an item you have recently bought. You can write about anything from purchasing a bike to purchasing a candy bar. As you write, watch for the errors discussed in this chapter. After you finish writing, revise to make your writing clearer.

UNIT 1 Editor's Checklist

Editing your work is an important step in the writing process. After you have completed your first draft, use this checklist to make sure that your work is clear and that it says what you want to say.

Use this checklist to help you assess your writing for sentence understanding.

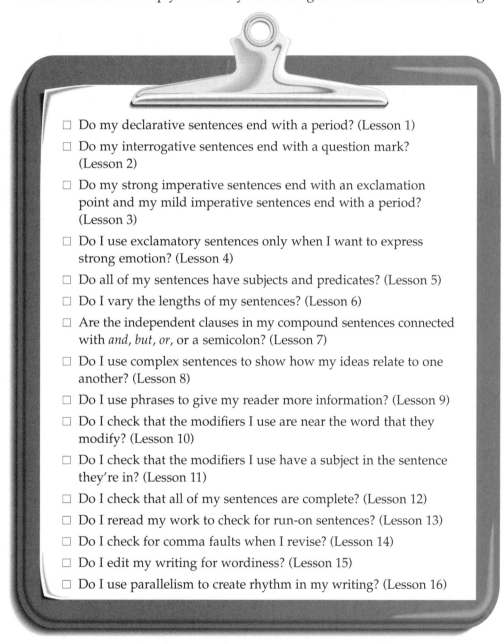

☐ Do my declarative sentences end with a period? (Lesson 1)

☐ Do my interrogative sentences end with a question mark? (Lesson 2)

☐ Do my strong imperative sentences end with an exclamation point and my mild imperative sentences end with a period? (Lesson 3)

☐ Do I use exclamatory sentences only when I want to express strong emotion? (Lesson 4)

☐ Do all of my sentences have subjects and predicates? (Lesson 5)

☐ Do I vary the lengths of my sentences? (Lesson 6)

☐ Are the independent clauses in my compound sentences connected with *and*, *but*, *or*, or a semicolon? (Lesson 7)

☐ Do I use complex sentences to show how my ideas relate to one another? (Lesson 8)

☐ Do I use phrases to give my reader more information? (Lesson 9)

☐ Do I check that the modifiers I use are near the word that they modify? (Lesson 10)

☐ Do I check that the modifiers I use have a subject in the sentence they're in? (Lesson 11)

☐ Do I check that all of my sentences are complete? (Lesson 12)

☐ Do I reread my work to check for run-on sentences? (Lesson 13)

☐ Do I check for comma faults when I revise? (Lesson 14)

☐ Do I edit my writing for wordiness? (Lesson 15)

☐ Do I use parallelism to create rhythm in my writing? (Lesson 16)

UNIT 1   What Have You Learned?

True or False
    In the blanks, write *T* for true and *F* for false.

1. _____ *The girl swam and her friend ate.* That is a simple sentence.

2. _____ *Wait for me!* That is an interrogative sentence.

3. _____ *Jimmy saw his profits disappear.* That is a declarative sentence.

4. _____ *Although it hurts, I'll keep playing.* That is a complex sentence.

5. _____ *You can pretend to be my teacher.* In that sentence, *can pretend to be my teacher* is the complete predicate.

Multiple Choice
    Write the letter of the problem in the blank before each sentence.

A. comma fault   B. run-on sentence   C. sentence fragment
D. wordiness   E. parallelism error   F. misplaced modifier

6. _____ Before we go.

7. _____ At the point in time we went, we had nothing.

8. _____ They left early, ate little, and drinking nothing.

9. _____ The chess player scowled, his opponent grinned.

10. _____ Conditions were dangerous he could not leave.

11. _____ A friendly nod pleased the man from his friend.

Revise
    Rewrite sentences 6–11 in order on the lines below, correcting the errors.

12. _____

13. _____

14. _____

15. _____

16. _____

17. _____

UNIT 2 Building Sentences

When you build sentences, you create complete thoughts that make sense to your reader. The more you know about the parts of a sentence, the more effective your sentences will be.

Define It

Writers must understand the parts of speech and how they work together. They must also be able to use grammar and punctuation so that they can effectively build sentences.

Understand It

How much do you already know about building sentences? Read these paragraphs. The first is correct, while the second has errors.

Example A

In 1961, a famous painting by Henri Matisse was hung at a New York museum. That wasn't so remarkable. What was remarkable was that for more than a month, the painting was hung upside down. The embarrassed director of the museum admitted the error and turned the painting right side up.

Example B

In 1961, a famous painting by Henri Matisse were hanged at a New York museums. It wasn't so remarkable. What was remarkable was that for more, than a month, the painting was hung upside down. The embarrassed Director of the Museum admits the error and turned the painting right side up.

Apply It

1. Use what you know about sentences to discuss Example A with a classmate. Decide why you think each sentence is correct.

2. Now discuss Example B. Which sentences are incorrect? How would you correct these sentences?

3. Fill out the first two columns in the chart below with what you know and what you want to know about grammar, mechanics, and usage. At the end of the unit, fill out the third column.

What I Know	What I Want to Know	What I Learned

CHAPTER 4   Understanding Grammar

The parts of speech are the building blocks of sentences. Every word in every sentence is a building block with a name. When you learn to recognize and identify the parts of speech, you'll find that putting together sentences is easier.

Define It

The **parts of speech** are the eight groups into which words can be classified. The eight parts of speech are: *nouns, verbs, pronouns, adjectives, adverbs, prepositions, conjunctions,* and *interjections*. Each of these parts of speech has a job.

Understand It

To identify a word's part of speech, you have to know the word's job in a sentence. The same word can take on different jobs in different sentences. When a word's job changes, so does its part of speech. In the examples below, see how a word can change its meaning—and its job—from sentence to sentence.

His **pants** are made of wool. (In this sentence, **pants** means a piece of clothing.)

The dog **pants** when it is hot. (In this sentence, **pants** means an action the dog takes.)

Apply It

▶   What do you already know about the parts of speech? Explain the different meanings of the word *show* in the sentences below.

The television **show** is boring.

Show me the answer to the question.

He plays **show** tunes with the school band.

1. What does *show* mean in the first sentence?

_____

2. What does *show* mean in the second sentence?

_____

3. What does *show* mean in the third sentence?

_____

Lesson 17 Nouns

Take a vampire, a volcano, a movie star, and a pig. What do they have in common? Every one is a noun.

Define It

A **noun** names a person, place, thing, or idea. Nouns are called **common nouns** if they name any person, place, thing, or idea. Common nouns do not begin with a capital letter unless they begin a sentence. Some examples of common nouns are *student*, *country*, *baseball*, and *happiness*.

Nouns are called **proper nouns** if they name a particular person, place, thing, or idea. Proper nouns begin with a capital letter. Some examples of proper nouns are *Juan*, *Broadway*, *River High*, and *Saturday*.

Compound nouns are made up of two or more words that act as one noun. Some examples of compound nouns are *Elm Street*, *New York City*, and *stop sign*. *Great-grandmother* is an example of a hyphenated compound noun.

Understand It

In the following sentences, the nouns are in **bold type**.

> **Jamal** paused before throwing the **ball** to **Jake**, who smashed a **home run** out of the **park**. (**Jamal** and **Jake** are proper nouns. **Ball**, **home run**, and **park** are common nouns. **Home run** is a compound noun.)

More About Nouns Often, the words *the*, *a*, or *an* appear before a noun. For example, We saw *a* movie in *the* theater about *an* elephant.

1. Underline the nouns in the following paragraph. Write a *C* above the common nouns, a *P* above the proper nouns, and a *CM* above the compound nouns.

> In the dim late-afternoon light, Lolly skied past the sign that said "Danger!" When her half-brother, Jim, saw she was nearing the edge of Black Gulch, he tried to grab her but missed. Just as she slid by him, Lolly grabbed a tree. For a few seconds, Jim could not move. Then he cupped his hands and yelled for help.

Apply It

2. Continue the story above by adding two or three more sentences on a separate sheet of paper. Underline the nouns you use.

Lesson 18   Verbs

A sentence can be complete without a subject. The imperative sentence *Go!* is an example. Without a verb, though, no sentence is complete.

Define It

A **verb** is the part of speech that shows action or a state of being. Here are examples of the most common kinds of verbs. The verbs are in **bold type**.

> Jaime **raced** toward the finish line. (The word **raced** is an action verb that shows movement or behavior.)
>
> Maura **was** the chosen one. (The word **was** is a linking verb that shows a state of being or a condition.)
>
> The drama coach **could speak** Japanese. (The word **could** is a helping verb. It helps the main verb **speak** to show an action.)

Understand It

In most sentences, the verb follows the subject. It is often the first part of the predicate of a sentence, as you can see in the first example below. In interrogative sentences, though, the predicate often comes before the subject. Notice that in the second example, the helping verb appears before the subject of the sentence and the action verb appears after the subject.

> We **won** the lottery.
>
> **Did** Stevie **finish** the mocha ice cream?

1. Underline the verbs in the following paragraph.

> Ron braced his feet against the starting block. He heard the crack of the gun, and he was off. Before he could catch his breath, Rashon was ahead of him. As he was passing Ron, Rashon looked back mockingly. When he crossed the finish line, Rashon threw his hands upward in joy.

Apply It

2. Verbs make your writing exciting by showing action. Find a piece of writing you have done recently and copy it onto another sheet of paper. If possible, change the verbs so that they show more action. Underline the verbs you use in your writing.

Lesson 19 Pronouns

Compare these two sentences. *Ming asked Ming's brother if Ming could borrow Ming's brother's bike. Ming asked her brother if she could borrow his bike.* What's the difference? Pronouns eliminated the repeated use of the words *Ming* and *Ming's brother*. They also helped link the words in the sentence.

Define It

A **pronoun** is a word that takes the place of a noun. Pronouns can refer to persons, places, ideas, or things without naming them. Pronouns can be singular or plural. Here is an overview of three kinds of pronouns: personal pronouns, possessive pronouns, and indefinite pronouns.

Personal pronouns refer to specific people or things.

Person	Singular	Plural
First Person	I, me	we, us
Second Person	you	you
Third Person	he, him, she, her, it	they, them

In the example below, the personal pronouns are in **bold type.**

If **you** climb the tree, **I** will be there when **it** breaks.

Possessive pronouns show ownership.

Person	Singular	Plural
First Person	my, mine	our, ours
Second Person	your, yours	your, yours
Third Person	his, her, hers, its	their, theirs

In the examples below, the possessive pronouns are in **bold type**.

If **your** mother is right, **her** glasses are on **my** nightstand.

There are many **indefinite pronouns**. They refer to persons, places, things, or ideas in general. Here are some examples.

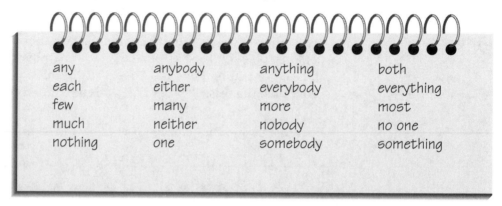

any	anybody	anything	both
each	either	everybody	everything
few	many	more	most
much	neither	nobody	no one
nothing	one	somebody	something

In the examples below, the indefinite pronouns are in **bold type**.

Nobody knows what **anybody** is doing.

Understand It

Use a pronoun to avoid repeating a noun over and over. Be careful, though, that it is clear which noun each pronoun replaces.

1. Try filling in the blanks below with the correct pronoun form.

Jeremy knew that _____ (him, he) was in big trouble.

Although _____ (his, him) friends had always saved _____ (his, him) before, today _____ (they, them) were nowhere in sight.

Apply It

2. Rewrite the following paragraph on another sheet of paper. Replace the nouns with pronouns to eliminate repeating a noun too many times.

Mim wanted Mim's speech to be perfect, so Mim practiced and practiced the speech. Finally, when Mim stood up before the club, Mim smiled. Mim knew Mim was about to give the best speech of Mim's life.

Lesson 20   Adjectives

Think of the contrast between a *sweet* orange and a *sour* orange. The adjective makes the difference. Adjectives add detail to your writing.

Define It

An **adjective** modifies a noun or pronoun. Adjectives answer the questions *What kind? How many?* and *Which?*

> Chou gave the child a **friendly** nod. (What kind of nod?)
>
> Elena saw **six** doves fly. (How many doves flew?)
>
> I'll take the **first** flight out. (Which flight will you take?)

Like most nouns, adjectives usually are capitalized only when they begin a sentence. **Proper adjectives**, though, which are formed from proper nouns, do begin with a capital letter.

> His **Chinese** friend taught him to cook. (**Chinese** is a proper adjective. It is formed from the proper noun **China**.)

More About Adjectives Before you choose an adjective, think carefully about the thing you're describing. Visualizing can help you paint a clear picture in your writing.

Understand It

1. On a separate sheet of paper, list the adjectives in these paragraphs. Next to each adjective, write the word or words that it modifies.

> The sweet smell of the South American meadow and the yellow sundews attract the butterflies. The butterflies fly into the deadly trap.
>
> The flowers release a gluey nectar that traps the butterflies. Next, they release a poisonous substance. Sundew plants, beautiful and deadly, are just one of the many kinds of plants that eat animals.

Apply It

2. Look out the window. On another sheet of paper, write a paragraph that describes what you see. Use adjectives that paint a clear picture.

Lesson 21   Adverbs

Like adjectives, adverbs modify other words. Without them, no one would be able to walk *slowly* or be *extremely* happy. Adverbs tell how things happen.

Define It

An **adverb** modifies a verb, an adjective, or another adverb. Adverbs answer the questions *How? When? Where? How often?* and *To what extent?*

■ In these examples, different adverbs modify the verb *danced*. The adverbs are in **bold type** and the arrows point to the word they modify.

> The prince danced **gracefully**. (How did he dance?)
>
> The prince danced **yesterday**. (When did he dance?)
>
> The prince danced **anywhere**. (Where did he dance?)
>
> The prince danced **often**. (How often did he dance?)
>
> The prince **barely** danced. (To what extent did he dance?)

More About Adverbs Many adverbs end with the letters *-ly*: *angrily, hopelessly, seemingly.* You can often change an adjective to an adverb by adding *-ly*: *eager, eagerly; beautiful, beautifully; great, greatly.*

■ Here is an example of an adverb modifying an adjective.

> The **somewhat** graceful prince danced. (How graceful was the prince? The adverb **somewhat** modifies the adjective **graceful**.)

■ Finally, here's an example of an adverb modifying another adverb.

> The prince danced **extremely** quickly. (How quickly did the prince dance? The adverb **extremely** modifies the adverb **quickly**.)

Understand It

1. Underline the adverbs in the following sentences. Draw an arrow from the adverb to the word it modifies. Use the examples on page 36 to help you.

> Slowly, the zookeeper advanced. "Now, I don't want any trouble," he muttered to the monkeys. He moved his hands carefully to the cage door.
>
> The monkeys hooted noisily. Somehow, they knew that the zookeeper was deathly afraid of them. Everywhere he went, the monkeys always followed him, and he was really getting tired of it.

Apply It

2. As you've learned, adverbs tell how things happen. On a separate sheet of paper, write the paragraphs below. Add adverbs to show *How? When? Where? How often?* and *To what extent?* in the story. Use the first sentence as an example.

> Sarah saw the finish line clearly. It hurt to breathe, but she told herself that she could keep going. This race was important. If she came in first, her school would win the championship. If she did not, she would be responsible for the defeat.
>
> Out of the corner of her eye, Sarah saw someone behind her. It was Bethany, the girl from East High. Bethany ran. Sarah heard the footfalls. She began to run. Every step hurt, but Sarah kept going. She would win.

3. Compare your paragraphs with those of another student. Underline the adverbs in the student's work. How did the adverbs that both of you used change the story? How did your stories differ because you used different adverbs?

Lesson 22   Prepositions

Prepositions connect a noun to another part of the sentence. They tell you that Ben's locker is *near* Lisa's. They tell you that the catsup is *behind* the mustard.

Define It

A **preposition** shows the relationship between a noun or pronoun and another word in a sentence.

- Prepositions can show location.

> That planet is **outside** the galaxy. (The preposition **outside** shows where the planet is in relation to the galaxy.)

- They can show direction.

> The asteroid is headed **toward** the sun. (**Toward** shows where the asteroid is going in relation to the sun.)

- They can show time.

> She lost her sunglasses **during** the eclipse. (**During** shows when she lost her sunglasses in relation to the eclipse.)

- They also can show relationship.

> His presentation came complete **with** slides. (**With** shows what he had in relation to his presentation.)

More About Prepositions Here's a list of some of the most frequently used prepositions: *about, above, across, after, against, along, among, around, at, before, behind, below, beneath, beside, between, by, down, during, except, for, from, in, into, like, near, of, off, on, over, past, since, through, to, under, until, up, upon, with,* and *without.*

A phrase is a group of words that does not have a subject and a predicate and cannot stand alone. A **prepositional phrase** is a group of two or more words that begins with a preposition and ends with a noun or pronoun. In these examples, the prepositional phrases are in **bold type**.

■ A prepositional phrase can have as few as two words. It can also be much longer.

> **Beyond the dark, unknown galaxies** and **throughout time,** the stars **in the sky** have held a fascination **for people.**

■ There are also **compound prepositions**. Such prepositions contain two or more words that work as a one-word preposition does: *according to, in back of, in front of, because of, up to, away from, in spite of,* and *out of.* Treat them as if they were one-word prepositions. In the following example, the compound preposition is in **bold type**.

> The chart **in front of** the room shows the stars.

Understand It

1. Fill in the blanks with one of the prepositional phrases below.

> in the morning   out the door   with luck   for his job
> down the stairs   with a start   during the evening
>
> _____, when Thom opened his eyes, he realized
>
> _____ that he was late _____.
>
> He raced _____, grabbed his coat, and sped
>
> _____. _____, he could stay
>
> _____ and finish his work.

Apply It

2. To see how often writers use prepositions, choose a paragraph from any book or magazine. Copy it on another sheet of paper and underline all the prepositions you find. You can use the list in the Tip on page 38 to help you.

Lesson 23 Conjunctions

Like prepositions, conjunctions join words or groups of words. But notice the difference between these two sentences: *Would you like the strawberries or the liver? Would you like the strawberries and the liver?* The difference is the conjunction. In the first sentence, the conjunction *or* gives you a choice between strawberries and liver. In the second sentence, the conjunction *and* asks if you want both foods.

Define It

Conjunctions join words, phrases, and clauses. There are several kinds of conjunctions.

Coordinating conjunctions link words, clauses, and phrases that have the same grammatical structure. Such conjunctions include *and, or, but, yet, so,* and *nor*. In the examples below, the conjunctions are in **bold type**.

> I swam in the fishpond, **but** no one seemed to mind. (The conjunction **but** links the two independent clauses **I swam in the fishpond** and **no one seemed to mind.**)
>
> The octopus **and** the shark floated to the top of the tank. (**And** links the nouns **octopus** and **shark**.)

Subordinating conjunctions join a dependent clause to an independent clause. You see them in complex sentences, which are made up of at least one independent and one dependent clause. Such conjunctions include *after, although, as, as if, because, before, for, if, once, since, so, so that, than, that, though, unless, until, when, whenever, where, whereas, wherever, whether,* and *while*.

> You were at the front desk **when** two starfish escaped. (The independent clause **You were at the front desk** and the dependent clause **when two starfish escaped** are linked by the subordinating conjuction **when**.)

Understand It

▶ Fill in the blanks with one of the conjunctions in parentheses.

1. The low temperature _____ (or, and) the approaching storm stopped us, _____ (but, and) we still considered going out.

2. Jayme _____ (and, but) Meg can finish the experiment.

3. _____ (Until, Because) we knew it would be cold, we put on our warm jackets.

4. Can you work for me this afternoon, _____ (and, or) should I find a substitute?

5. We paid more, _____ (unless, but) we didn't mind _____ (and, because) the concert was worth it.

▶ In these sentences, underline the conjunctions.

6. Because we had forgotten the fish food, we had some hungry fish in the tank.

7. When you go to the river, you should see if the tadpoles are still there.

8. The shrimp and the jellyfish were hard to see in the murky water.

9. Finding a new species and proving it is new are very different things.

10. Those fish are not usually attacked because other fish know they are poisonous.

Apply It

11. Rewrite the following paragraphs on another sheet of paper. Be sure to connect the words, phrases, clauses, and sentences with conjunctions when appropriate.

> In the 1800s, people became interested in ancient temples. They became interested in ancient pyramids. Some traveled to Egypt. They tried to bring treasures back. Some of the visitors were archaeologists. Other visitors were bounty hunters. They wanted the treasures to sell. They wanted mummies to sell.
>
> Today, archaeologists find few treasures. Most have been found. Some have been stolen. Many of the ancient temples remain. They still amaze visitors.

12. On a separate sheet of paper, revise a piece of writing you have done so that it uses conjunctions correctly. If you prefer, you may write a new piece instead. Underline the conjunctions you use.

Lesson 24   Interjections

Wow! If you really want to show how you feel, use an interjection.

Define It

An **interjection** is a word or expression that shows surprise or strong feeling. It is not connected to any other word in the sentence. When an interjection is used within a sentence, it may be followed by a comma, a question mark, or an exclamation point.

> **Help!** My hands are too slippery to hold this.
>
> **Oh no**, that's my briefcase in the puddle.
>
> You won the contest? **Wow!**

More About Interjections Be careful how you use interjections. While a few add spice to writing, too many interjections can interrupt your reader's train of thought.

Understand It

Use one of the interjections below to fill in the blanks in the following sentences.

What   Stop   Oh, no   Wow   Great

1. _____! Look at all that bologna!

2. _____! The lettuce is the kind I like.

3. _____? Are we really out of mustard?

4. _____, I can't go a step farther without some lunch.

5. _____! The hungriest person I know is headed this way.

Apply It

6. On another sheet of paper, write a short, two-character dialogue about a natural event such as an earthquake or a tornado. In your dialogue, be sure to use interjections.

1. The following paragraphs contain errors in the uses of the parts of speech. There are also sentences that could be rephrased or combined so they read more smoothly. On another sheet of paper, rewrite the paragraphs eliminating the errors and rephrasing as needed.

"Hey! Either I'm crazy. That's a bear by those dumpsters." Esther looked. Wow! Amazing! Slow the Bear came, and the two girls stood, telling herself It might go away.

"It's coming closer, but I know. We're in no danger," Esther told hers friend Sue. Esther knew bears was as scared. Of they as it was of themselves. But yikes! How scary!

Them waited but the bear by them walking. Esther held its breath.

"It's gone. Are you all right?" it said. To her friend. "Was a close one."

2. On the lines below, write a paragraph about one activity you like to do on weekends. Your paragraph should contain examples of all eight parts of speech. Label at least two examples of each part of speech in your writing.

_____

_____

_____

_____

_____

CHAPTER 5   Using the Parts of Speech

Now that you can identify the parts of speech, you are closer to being able to use them correctly. From using the right verb tense to finding the right pronoun, this chapter can help you learn to make your writing more precise and understandable to your reader.

Define It

One way to tell if you are using a part of speech correctly is to trust your ear. If you read something that doesn't sound right, take a closer look. Check if you used the wrong verb or the wrong pronoun. Look at the punctuation. If you have questions, ask a classmate, family member, or your teacher to read your work and make suggestions for revisions.

Understand It

▶ Use your ear to tell you where the problems are in the sentences below. Revise them so they sound correct to you.

1. That was the worstest movie I've ever seen.

_____

2. We go to the movies last Thursday.

_____

3. Him and me bought popcorn without butter.

_____

4. We got the bestest seats in the theater—the front row!

_____

5. Do you think us could go again next week?

_____

Apply It

6. Compare your answers with a classmate. If you have different answers, discuss why you made the changes you did.

Lesson 25   Basic Verb Tenses

Did the cat catch the mouse already? Is she catching it now? Will she catch the mouse later? What's different in these questions is the *time* of the action.

Define It

A verb's **tense** shows the reader the time of the action or the state of being that is being described.

Understand It

There are three basic tenses: past, present, and future. You can see a verb's tense through the verb's form. Look at the differences among these three sentences. The verbs are in **bold type**.

> Mark **helped** his sister. (The past tense of the verb **help** is **helped**. It shows that the action has already happened.)
>
> Mark **helps** his sister. (The present tense of the verb **help** is **helps**. It shows that the action is happening now.)
>
> Mark **will help** his sister. (The future tense of the verb **help** is **will help**. It shows that the action will happen in the future.)

As you can see, the verb's tense shows you that the *time* when Mark helps his sister changes.

▶ Underline the verbs in each of the following sentences. Write each verb's tense on the lines. Use the examples above to help you.

1. They will walk to the store. _____

2. I decided to go by myself. _____

3. Antarctica is very cold in July. _____

4. How many people does he know? _____

Apply It

5. On the lines below, write a sentence that tells what you are doing now. Revise the sentence, using the past tense. Revise it once more, using the future tense.

_____

_____

_____

Lesson 26   Regular Verbs

I talked to Pete yesterday, I am talking to him now, and I will talk to him later.
How do you know that the speaker has been talking to Pete for a long time? The verb *talk* takes different forms to show you the change of time.

Define It

In most tenses, a **regular verb** changes its form depending on its subject's person and number.

Understand It

Present Tense

The list below uses the verb *talk* to show how regular verbs change form in the **present tense**.

PERSON	SINGULAR	PLURAL
First	I talk	we talk
Second	you talk	you talk
Third	he/she/it talks	they talk

More About Verbs In regular verbs, only the third person singular changes. (For example, he *talks*, but I *talk*, you *talk*, and we, you, and they *talk*.) To make the third person singular, just add *-s* to any regular verb.

Present Participle

Another form of regular present tense verbs is called the **present participle**. This form adds *-ing* to the present tense verb and takes a helping verb like *is* or *are*. The present participle of *talk* is *is talking* or *are talking*.

Past Tense

To form the past tense of a regular verb, add *-ed* or *-d* to the present tense.

PERSON	SINGULAR	PLURAL
First	I talked	we talked
Second	you talked	you talked
Third	he/she/it talked	they talked

Past Participle

Like the present tense, the past tense also has a participle. To form the **past participle**, add the words *have*, *has*, or *had* before the past tense verb. The past participle of *talking* is *has talked*, *had talked*, or *have talked*.

These four forms (the present, present participle, past, and past participle) are also known as the **principal parts of the verb**.

Future Tense

For the future tense, add the word *will* before the verb.

PERSON	SINGULAR	PLURAL
First	I will talk	we will talk
Second	you will talk	you will talk
Third	he/she/it will talk	they will talk

▶ Fill in the blank with the correct form of the verb in parentheses. Use the tense given.

1. She _____ (visit, *past tense*) colleges last year.

2. Next month, he _____ (apply, *future tense*) for the scholarship.

3. We already _____ (interview, *past participle*) at that campus.

4. Jamey _____ (call, *present participle*) the high school to get his records.

5. I'll have to work hard all summer if I _____ (decide, *present tense*) to go to the state college.

Apply It

6. Write a paragraph that compares your ideas about careers when you were a child with your ideas now. Use at least one example of the present, present participle, past, past participle, and future in your writing. Underline and label the tenses you use.

Lesson 27   Irregular Verbs

Most verbs in English are regular verbs. Regular verbs form their tenses in a predictable way. Irregular verbs, though, follow no predictable pattern.

Define It

An **irregular verb** does not follow a predictable pattern when it moves from the present, present participle, past, and past participle forms of the verb. You will have to memorize the irregular verbs, but you are already familiar with many of them. Here are examples of how the irregular verb *begin* changes its forms. You can see that *begin* does not make its past tense and past participle forms by adding *-ed* or *-d*. The verbs are in **bold type**.

> I **begin** to sing. (The present tense of **begin** is **begin**.)
>
> I **began** to sing. (The past tense of **begin** is **began**.)
>
> I **had begun** to sing. (The past participle form of **begin** is **had begun**.)

Understand It

Here are some of the most common ways for irregular verbs to form tenses.

	Present	Past	Past Participle
changing vowels	begin	began	begun
	sing	sang	sung
changing vowels in past, but adding **-en** in past participle	drive	drove	driven
	give	gave	given
changing **-ee** to **-e**	flee	fled	fled
	bleed	bled	bled
changing **-d** to **-t**	build	built	built
	lend	lent	lent
same present and past participle	come	came	come
	run	ran	run
same past and past participle	bring	brought	brought
	think	thought	thought
making no change	cut	cut	cut

Here is a list of some common irregular verbs.

Present	Past	Past Participle
bite	bit	bit or bitten
choose	chose	chosen
do	did	done
eat	ate	eaten
get	got	got or gotten
give	gave	given
go	went	gone
know	knew	known
leave	left	left
say	said	said
see	saw	seen
take	took	taken
throw	threw	thrown
write	wrote	written

▶ Fill in the blanks with the correct form of the verbs in parentheses. In some cases, you can choose which tense to use.

1. I _____ (sing) in the concert last night.

2. They had _____ (go) to the concert.

3. My cousin _____ (take) her opera glasses and _____ (see) the stage better.

4. If you _____ (know) what I _____ (see) there, you would be surprised.

Apply It

5. On another sheet of paper, rewrite the following paragraph to eliminate the errors with irregular verbs.

> When he see that opera star, he knowed she was something special. She weared a beautiful white gown and standed up there like a queen. Then she begun to sing. She singed like an angel. Later, when we had went from the theater, I seen her left. She blowed me a kiss.

Lesson 28   Verb Tense Consistency

■ ■

What is the difference between these two sentences? *Marque says he is angry.* *Marque says he was angry.* In the first sentence, Marque is angry now. In the second sentence, he was angry before, but he is not angry now. Choosing the correct verb tenses can help you say what you mean.

Define It

Verb tense consistency means being sure that your verbs show the correct time relationship to one another. For example, if two actions occur at the same time, you need to use the same tense in your description. Here is an example of a verb whose tenses are not consistent.

> *Inconsistent:* We **will bring** the umbrellas to the beach, and Frank **brought** the food. (The future and past tenses are mixed.)
>
> *Consistent:* We **will bring** the umbrellas to the beach, and Frank **will bring** the food. (Both verbs are in the future tense.)

Sometimes, though, the action in a sentence needs to move from the past to the present, or from the present to the future. This shift can show how one action causes another action. When this happens, the verb tense needs to shift, too.

> After we **finish** the chicken, I **will put** the bones in the garbage. (The first action, **finish**, occurs in the present. The second action, **will put**, will occur in the future.)
>
> I **sang** to the seagulls, and now they **want** an encore. (The first action, **sang**, occurred in the past. The second action, **want**, occurs in the present.)

Understand It

In most writing, it's wise to use the same tense, or time. Your writing will be clearer and more focused. Look at the difference between these two sentences.

> *Inconsistent:* Ray **saw** Angela was there, and he **walks** eagerly up to her. (It's unclear when Ray walked up to Angela.)
>
> *Consistent:* Ray **saw** Angela was there, and he **walked** eagerly up to her. (It's clear that Ray walked up to Angela at the same time as he saw her.)

▶ Change the verb tenses in these sentences to make them consistent. Write the new sentences on the lines below.

1. Jamie tells Sue what to do, and Sue did what he wanted.

_____

2. As the sun heated the beach, I will put on my sunscreen.

_____

3. You fry the fish, and we walked on the beach.

_____

4. That robin sings sadly yesterday as I watched it.

_____

Apply It

5. There are errors in verb tense consistency in this paragraph. Rewrite it on the lines below, correcting the errors.

I took a tour of a newspaper office last month. While I was there, I see reporters bustling about, working on a story about a beached whale. They talked fast and walk faster. Photographers are rushing about, too, showing me lots of great pictures. I got wrapped up in the excitement, and for a while, I really want to be a newspaper reporter myself.

_____

_____

_____

_____

_____

_____

Lesson 29   Direct and Indirect Objects

Direct and indirect objects can tell you more about the verb in a sentence. Compare these two sentences. *Randi dropped. Randi dropped the anchor.* Because of the direct object *the anchor*, you know what Randi dropped.

Define It

The **direct object** of the verb is a word or group of words that receives the action of the verb. It answers the question *what?* or *whom?* about a verb. In the example above, the direct object *the sea* answers the question *what did we sail?* In the example below, the direct object is in **bold type**.

> We forgot **the sails**. (What did we forget? We forgot the sails.)

The **indirect object** of the verb answers the questions *to what?* and *for whom?* about the verb. It is used with verbs of telling, asking, and receiving (*give, offer, bring, take, lend, send,* and *buy* are examples). In the following example, the indirect object is in **bold type**.

> He gave **the sailor** a new net. (To whom did he give the net? He gave the net to the sailor.)

 More About Indirect Objects A quick way to identify an indirect object is to add the word *to* or *for* in front of the word(s) you think might be the indirect object. If the sentence makes sense after this addition, the word is an indirect object: He gave *to* the sailor a new net.

In the following example, the direct objects are underlined with one line and the indirect objects are underlined with two lines.

> Rex offered his <u>paw</u>. (What did Rex offer? He offered his paw.)
>
> Rex offered <u>Charlene</u> his paw. (To whom did Rex offer his paw? He offered his paw to Charlene.)

Understand It

▶ In the following sentences, underline the direct object once. Underline the indirect object twice. There may be more than one direct object and indirect object in a sentence. Some sentences may not have an indirect object.

1. Someday we will cruise the Indian Ocean.

2. Before you rig the sails, please give Barney the end of the rope.

3. He wrote *Seven Years Before the Mast.*

4. She sailed that boat and never gave anyone trouble.

5. Should I lend them my new boat?

6. Jackson tried to show the crew the ropes, but they ignored him.

Apply It

7. Underline the direct objects once and the indirect objects twice in the following paragraph.

We called the sailor Mr. Danger after he told us his story.

He said it was a calm night at sea when suddenly an angry shark began

hitting the boat again and again. Before long, panicked sailors threw

themselves into lifeboats. That, of course, only made things worse.

8. Now complete this story on the lines below, using direct and indirect objects in your writing. Underline the direct objects once and the indirect objects twice.

_____

_____

_____

_____

_____

_____

_____

_____

_____

Lesson 30   Subject and Object Pronouns

Who is on the phone? Is it *him*? Is it *he*? Knowing the difference between subject and object pronouns can help you answer the question correctly.

Define It

A pronoun is used in its **subject** or **object** form depending on its job in the sentence. The subject form acts as the subject of a verb. The object form acts as the object of a verb. Here are examples of subject and object pronouns. The pronouns are in **bold type**.

> I asked the dog to sit. (Because the pronoun I is the subject of the sentence, it is a subject pronoun.)
>
> I asked **him** to sit. (Because the pronoun **him** is the object of the verb, it is an object pronoun.)

Here is a list of the subject and object pronouns. To choose the right pronoun, first decide if the pronoun is a subject or an object in the sentence, as in the examples above. Then decide if the pronoun refers to a singular person or thing or to a plural person or thing.

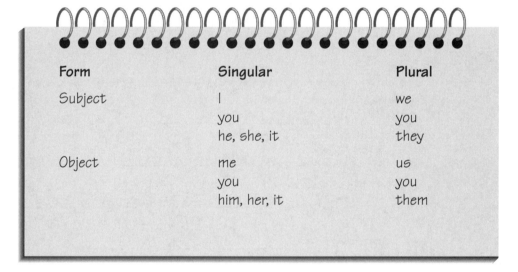

Form	Singular	Plural
Subject	I	we
	you	you
	he, she, it	they
Object	me	us
	you	you
	him, her, it	them

Understand It

Most of the misunderstandings about these pronouns occur in compounds: *he and I, you and me, you and I*. The pronouns in the following examples are in **bold type**.

> **She and I** trained the dog. (Because **she and I** is a compound subject, the pronouns should both be in the subject form.)
>
> He took **her and me** to the dog show. (Because **her and me** is a compound direct object, the pronouns should both be in the object form.)

TIP **More About Compound Pronouns** If you can't decide which form to use, take away one of the pronouns. Consider the examples you just read: *She* trained the dog. *I* trained the dog. He took *her* to the dog show. He took *me* to the dog show.

These pronouns can also be confusing when they are part of a prepositional phrase.

> Between **you** and **me**, that bulldog is out of control. (The pronouns **you** and **me** are the objects of the preposition **between**.)

▶ Circle the correct pronoun choice in the following sentences.

1. Do you think (us, we) are ready for the show?

2. (He and I, Him and me) thought the poodle deserved the award.

3. Please tell (her and me, she and me) what you have in mind.

4. (Jim and I, Jim and me) agreed that the arena was shabby.

5. That dog was so strong it pulled (she, her) off the path.

6. I believe that between (you and I, you and me) we can decide on a winner.

Apply It

7. Cross out the pronoun mistakes in the following paragraph and write the correct word above each one.

> Let Gene and me tell you and her about poodles. First, when he and me went to Europe last year, him and I found out that poodles first came from Germany. Did you know that? Also, a poodle breeder told he and I that there are three kinds of poodles: toy, miniature, and standard.

Lesson 31 Adjectives and Adverbs that Compare

Amy's good at sprints. Marta's better at sprints. Jana's the best at sprints. The words you use to compare things show your reader how strongly you feel.

Define It

Comparing adjectives and adverbs is a matter of **degree**. The **positive degree** describes one thing (*good*). The **comparative degree** compares two things (*better*). The **superlative degree** compares more than two things (*best*). Here are some rules for creating adjectives and adverbs that compare.

■ Most adjectives or adverbs with one syllable add *-er* and *-est*.

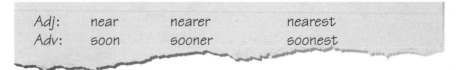

| Adj: | near | nearer | nearest |
| Adv: | soon | sooner | soonest |

■ Most adjectives or adverbs that end in *-y* change the *-y* to *-i*, and add *-er* and *-est*.

| Adj: | sleepy | sleepier | sleepiest |
| Adv: | early | earlier | earliest |

■ Some adjectives and adverbs add the words *more* and *most*.

| Adj: | alert | more alert | most alert |
| Adv: | quickly | more quickly | most quickly |

■ Like verbs, some adjectives and adverbs have irregular forms. If you're unsure which form to use, check your dictionary.

| Adj: | good | better | best |
| Adv: | well | better | best |

Understand It

Use the correct form of the adjective in parentheses to fill in the blanks.

1. She was the (nice) —————— of the three cheerleaders.

2. Sam did that (well) —————— than his brother.

Apply It

3. On another sheet of paper, write a letter to a friend comparing two places you know. Use the three degrees of adjectives and adverbs.

Lesson 32   Subject-Verb Agreement

Subjects and verbs must work together. If someone said to you, "Birds flies," what would you think? You might think he was talking about two flying animals, and you might expect him to say, "Birds, flies, and bees . . ." You might also think that he was talking about birds flying and assume that he'd used the wrong verb. In either case, you'd be confused.

Define It

Subjects and verbs **agree** when they are both either singular or plural. A singular subject names one person, place, or thing; a plural subject names more than one person, place, or thing.

> **Amy cooks** great food. (Both the subject, **Amy**, and the verb, **cooks**, are singular.)
>
> The **cousins cook** great food. (Both the subject, **cousins**, and the verb, **cook**, are plural.)

Understand It

A few simple rules can make subject-verb agreement easy to understand.

Phrases

Sometimes, phrases come between the subject and verb. This can make keeping track of subject-verb agreement difficult. The trick is to disregard the phrase(s) and think of only the subject and verb.

> **The cousins**, who live in Los Angeles, **cook** great food. (When you disregard the phrase **who live in Los Angeles**, you have **The cousins cook** great food.)

Compound Subjects

- A compound subject connected by *and* takes a plural verb.

> **Judy and LaShawn prepare** the main course. (The compound subject **Judy and LaShawn** takes the plural verb **prepare**.)

- An exception to this is when the compound subject acts as a unit.

> **Macaroni and cheese is** on the menu. (**Macaroni and cheese**, the subject, takes the singular verb **is**.)

- Compound subjects joined by *or* take a verb that agrees with the closest subject.

> Either Andrea or **my friends are making** the brownies.
> (The closest subject is **my friends,** so the verb is the plural **are.**)

Collective Nouns

- Collective nouns (*team, group, class*) may take either a singular or plural verb, depending on how the noun is used. If the sentence sounds odd, though, rewrite it.

> The **audience claps** wildly. (The **audience** acts as a unit.)
>
> The **audience put** on their coats and left. (The **audience** acted as individuals.)
>
> Better: The **people** in the audience **put** on their coats and left.

Indefinite pronouns

- Indefinite pronouns refer to people and things in general. Some are always singular, such as *everyone, neither, no one,* and *something.* They take a singular verb. Other indefinite pronouns are always plural, such as *few, both,* and *several.*

> **No one knows** what to do. (**No one** is singular.)
>
> **Few drink** tea. (**Few** is plural.)

- Some indefinite pronouns can be either singular or plural (*all, any, enough, more, most, none, plenty,* and *some*). They are singular when they refer to a single person (or group), place, or thing. They are plural when they refer to two or more.

> **All** of the dinner **was** delicious. (**All** refers to the entire dinner, which is singular.)
>
> **All** of the meals **were** delicious. (**All** refers to the meals, which are plural.)

▶ In the following sentences, underline the subject and circle the verb that agrees with it.

1. The chef and the owner (is, are) planning a new restaurant.

2. Either you or Fred (fries, fry) the potatoes.

3. Some of the diners (is, are) planning to order fish.

4. Ms. Polumbo and I (decorates, decorate) the cake.

5. Several workers (forget, forgets) what the job is.

6. The class (cook, cooks) the meal tonight.

Apply It

7. Choose the verb that agrees with the subject to fill in the blank. Then continue the story on a separate sheet of paper. Make sure your subjects and verbs agree.

To make money for the class trip, Malin _____ (told, tell)

the class members that they should make a chocolate chip cookie

big enough to set a world record. Everyone who paid would

_____ (gets, get) to eat it. No one _____ (know,

knew) what the rules for world records were, though, so first some-

one had to _____ (went, go) to the library to look in the

Guinness Book of World Records.

"You won't believe this," Janet _____ (say, said) when she

returned. "The record cookie has three million chocolate chips."

Malin _____ (looked, look) at the class. "Well," he

_____ (says, said),

Lesson 33   Pronoun Agreement

Making pronouns agree can be a puzzle. Should the sentence read: *Everyone lost his way* or *Everyone lost their way?* These pronouns confuse many writers, but there is a way through this maze.

Define It

The **antecedent** of a pronoun is the word to which the pronoun refers.

> Madge knew **her** mother was coming. (**Madge** is the antecedent of **her.**)

Pronouns must agree with their antecedents when the two match in number. This can be easy, as in the sentence above. You know that *her* refers to Madge.

Understand It

Pronouns must agree with their antecedents in three ways.

- **Number** shows whether the pronoun is singular or plural. A pronoun must agree in number with its antecedent. In the examples below, the pronoun and its antecedent are in **bold type**.

> **Fred** packed **his** suitcase. (Because **Fred** is a singular antecedent, it takes the singular pronoun **his.**)
>
> **They** packed **their** suitcases. (Because **they** is a plural antecedent, it takes the plural pronoun **their.**)

When you have two or more singular antecedents joined by *and*, use a plural pronoun.

> **Lan and Ed** think **they** are ready. (**Lan and Ed** are two singular antecedents joined by **and.**)

Indefinite pronouns refer to unknown persons or things. They are usually singular. Examples of pronouns that are always singular include *anybody*, *much*, and *either*. Other indefinite pronouns are always plural. Examples include *both*, *few*, and *many*. Some can be either singular or plural. Examples include *all* and *some*.

> When **someone** packed, **he** forgot the dishes. (**Someone** is the singular antecedent of the pronoun **he.**)

> Few know what **they** are doing. (**Few** is the plural antecedent of the pronoun **they**.)
>
> **Most** of the luggage has lost **its** newness. (**Luggage** is the singular antecedent of the pronoun **its**.)
>
> **Most** of the suitcases have lost **their** newness. (**Suitcases** is the plural antecedent of the pronoun **their**.)

- **Gender** shows whether the pronoun is male, female, or neuter. *Neuter* means "no gender." *He*, *him*, and *his* are masculine; *she*, *her*, and *hers* are feminine; and *it* and *its* are neuter. A pronoun must agree in gender with its antecedent.

> **Bob** told **his** mother to pack. (Both **Bob** and **his** are the masculine gender.)

Often, it is hard to tell the gender of the antecedent. This can happen with indefinite pronouns and with nouns. One solution is to use *his or her* or *he or she*. Another solution is to rewrite the sentence.

> A **park ranger** should do **his or her** best to answer questions. (**Park ranger** and **his or her** are singular.)
>
> **Park rangers** should do **their** best to answer questions. (**Park rangers** and **their** are plural.)
>
> **No one** should pretend **he or she** doesn't understand. (Both **no one** and **he or she** are singular.)
>
> **People** shouldn't pretend **they** don't understand. (**People** and **they** are plural.)

- **Person** shows whether a noun or pronoun is in the first person (the speaker), second person (the person being spoken to), or third person (the person or thing being spoken about). A pronoun must agree in person with its antecedent.

> I hate **my** alarm clock. (The pronouns **I** and **my** are in the first person.)
>
> Will **you** get **your** passport? (**You** and **your** are in the second person.)
>
> **Flo** eats **her** cereal. (**Flo** and **her** are in the third person.)

▶ Fill in the blank with a pronoun that agrees with each antecedent.

1. Evonne dropped _____ backpack.

2. When Janine and the others arrive, tell _____ to nap.

3. Everyone will bring _____ favorite book.

4. If you see a clerk, ask _____ to come here.

5. When the woman told Peter to move, _____ ignored _____.

Apply It

6. On the lines below, rewrite the following paragraphs so the pronouns agree with their antecedents. Not every pronoun needs correction.

> The class had planned their trip for months. Now everyone was so excited that they couldn't calm down. Some people got out his maps. A few people did a last-minute check of their tickets.
>
> Francie and Tim sat by himself and looked at the pictures of Brazil. Both were thinking that they were lucky to be going on such a trip.
>
> They was a good group, and it had worked hard, Francie thought. The members of the class were on its way.

_____

_____

_____

_____

_____

_____

_____

_____

Lesson 34   Clear Pronoun Reference

When I put a new lens in the telescope, it broke. Did the lens or the telescope break? You can't tell.

Define It

Using **clear pronoun references** can make your writing strong. Here is an example of a clear connection between an antecedent and a pronoun. The pronoun and its antecedent are in **bold type**.

> We saw the **shooting star** when **it** blazed across the sky.
> (**Shooting star** is clearly the antecedent of **it**.)

Here are examples of unclear antecedents. Rewriting can solve these problems.

> *Unclear*: Bob couldn't do **it**. (Bob couldn't do what?)
> *Clear*: Bob couldn't **fix the flat tire**.
>
> *Unclear*: Although June saw her teacher last week, **she** did not know **she** won the election. (Who did not know? Who won the election?)
> *Clear*: Although June saw her teacher last week, **she** did not know **her teacher** had won the election.

Understand It

▶ On another sheet of paper, rewrite these sentences so they are clear.

1. The astronomer wrote to the student before he became famous.

2. We trust the star chart and the telescope, but it sometimes lets us down.

3. If Jan and Sally are late, it will be because she had to watch the comet.

Apply It

4. On another sheet of paper, rewrite the following paragraph so the pronouns have clear antecedents. Replace pronouns that have unclear antecedents with appropriate substitutes when necessary.

> Comets were omens of doom in ancient times; they even appeared on their ancient tapestries. Two of the best-known comets are Halley's and Hale-Bopp. It is clear that it is a dramatic sight—there it is, sparkling in the sky. It is thrilling to see it.

1. The following paragraphs contain errors using the parts of speech. There are also sentences that could be reworked so they read better. On another sheet of paper, rewrite the paragraphs so the errors are eliminated and the sentences read more smoothly.

Jake and me setted off for our jungle adventure with our guide.

We thinks he is the bestest guide we have ever used. The scaryiest thing in the entirely trip happens right away. Him and I seen the most largest snake gliding toward him. It moves real slow. Then it flicked their tongue.

"Quick! Move!" our guide told we, and him and I do. Another second and there would have been nothing we could have did. That snake would have been on top of him and I.

After that, though, the trip going smooth. We seen colorfully birds, the beautifulest birds us had ever sawed. Him and I remember that trip for the rest of our lives.

2. Choose a time in the future in which you would like to live. On another sheet of paper, write how the world would look, why you would like to live in that time, and what you think living then would be like. When you have finished, edit your work, paying close attention to the ways you used the parts of speech. Rewrite your essay, correcting any errors you find.

CHAPTER **6** Understanding Mechanics

Once you know the parts of speech and how to use them, you can concentrate on learning how to use punctuation—periods, semicolons, hyphens, and the other marks—correctly.

Define It

The term for the usage of punctuation marks, capitalization, and italics is **mechanics**. Like correct usage, correct mechanics make your writing clearer for your reader.

Understand It

▶ Find out how much you know about mechanics. Revise the following sentences to correct the mistakes in using different sorts of punctuation. There are also problems with other areas of mechanics.

1. I liked the first book with nancy drew as the detective, which was called The Secret of the Old Clock.

_____

_____

2. tims' mom only like's to read biographies.

_____

_____

3. Everyone, who is a good reader, knows where the library is?

_____

_____

4. sharma should read that Book about Wild Animals.

_____

_____

Apply It

5. With a classmate, discuss the changes you made and why you made them. Explain each change and how it affects the sentence.

Lesson 35   Capitalization

my Sister Jenny told me that the Best Time she had ever had was hiking up Blue Sky Mountain. When you read that sentence, you probably stopped at some point because you were confused by the capitals. When you use capitals correctly, they help your reader navigate through a sentence.

Define It

Capitalization has two main purposes: to mark the beginning of a sentence and to show proper nouns.

Understand It

Capital letters work as signals. They show you when a new thought is being introduced. They also show you that a particular person, place, or thing is being discussed. Here are the rules for capitalization.

- Capitalize the first word in a sentence.

> **Since** you left, we haven't been to the movies.

- Capitalize proper nouns and adjectives.

> **Jacob** met the **English** actor **Mr. Grimshaw** at the **Atlantic Theater** in **New York**.

- Capitalize the first word of a sentence that is directly quoted.

> "**Do** I have the part?" asked the actor. "**You** know I want it."

When a quote is continued, do not capitalize the second part.

> "**I've** rehearsed my part for weeks," Gary said, "and still I can't remember my lines."

- Capitalize specific geographic areas. Do not capitalize general directions.

> We left the **East** and headed west.

■ Capitalize the names of monuments and well-known places.

> The **West Bank** in **Paris** is a well-known tourist spot.

■ Capitalize titles only when they appear in front of names.

> **Senator Jason** told the prime minister that the governor of Arkansas would come to the show.

▶ On another sheet of paper, rewrite the following sentences using correct capitalization.

1. if the governor of south dakota wants to come, Let him.

2. yesterday, maura and i saw the Eastern parking lot fill up.

3. the president said, "we have nothing to lose. Let us move forward."

4. "the grand canyon is beautiful," the japanese prime minister said, "and I want to return."

5. the city councilwoman, who is also a doctor, told us to be sure we brought enough water when we visited the gobi desert.

6. travelers to the southwest should not miss santa fe, new mexico.

7. although the captain was aware that the north star was clouded over, he knew by his compass which way was North.

8. "my dear friend," mr. gerson, the principal, said, "You have no reason to doubt me."

Apply It

9. Imagine you are telling your best friend about one special event in your life. On another sheet of paper, write what you would say about the place and the people, as well as the event. Be sure to mention why the event was special to you. Include some dialogue, if possible.

Lesson 36   Periods

hurry home stop treasure has been found stop you are rich stop

In the years before faxes and telephones, telegraphs carried information across the country quickly. Because there were no codes for punctuation marks, the word *stop* showed where periods should be.

Define It

The main job of a **period** is to end a declarative sentence. Periods can also end imperative sentences. Periods tell readers where to pause in their reading.

> The store is on the corner. Please go there.

Understand It

Periods also are sometimes needed inside sentences.

■ Use a period with initials in someone's name.

> M. L. Jones, Jr.

■ Use periods with most abbreviations, except post office abbreviations of states.

> P.O. Box 86, Stringville, CO U.S.A.

1. Add periods to punctuate this sentence correctly.

> Yesterday, Dr D L Grane, an M D from St Paul, left the United States When U S government officials heard about this, they went to his P O box In it was a letter postmarked N Y and addressed to his partner, Dr M Berger

Apply It

2. Think of someone to whom you might write, such as a grandparent or a friend who has moved away. On a separate sheet of paper, write a postcard to that person. Then write the person's address. Check your work, correcting any misuse of periods.

Lesson 37   Question Marks and Exclamation Points

Question marks and exclamation points are clues. They can tell you
what kind of a sentence you have read. They can also tell you if the writer
wanted to show uncertainty or strong feeling.

Define It

The job of a **question mark** is to end an interrogative sentence. Like a period,
a question mark also tells your reader to pause.

> What are you doing**?**

An **exclamation point** ends an exclamatory sentence, a forceful imperative
sentence, and a strong interjection.

> I can't believe that happened! (exclamatory sentence)
>
> Go to your room right now! (forceful imperative sentence)
>
> Wow! (strong interjection)

 More About Exclamation Points If exclamation points are
overused, they lose their impact.

Understand It

1. Change the periods in the following sentences to question marks and
   exclamation points where appropriate.

> Oh, no. Look at this. Bucky, did you do this. I know that expres-
> sion. Bucky, you are a bad dog. Come here this instant. I know you
> must have been hungry, but that's no reason to get into the
> garbage. It's a mess. What were you thinking. Don't cower in the
> corner like that. Don't you know the trouble you've caused me. The
> whole team is coming over here for a party in ten minutes. That's
> right, ten minutes. I wish you were a person. Then I would make you
> clean all this up.

Apply It

2. Look through magazine and newspaper ads. Find examples of appropriate
   and inappropriate uses of exclamation points and question marks. Copy
   them or paste them to a sheet of paper. Write why you think each is an
   appropriate or inappropriate use of these two punctuation marks.

Lesson 38　Commas

. . . .

Think of a comma as a pause in your writing. If you were reading your work aloud, you'd take a short breath when you saw a comma. Commas also help your reader arrange your words into meaningful groups.

Define It

The job of the **comma** is to group the parts of a sentence. Unlike periods, commas are used within sentences, not at the end of sentences.

What's the difference between these two sentences?

> The group without a drummer was boring.
>
> The group, without a drummer, was boring.

When you read the first sentence, you don't pause when you reach the phrase *without a drummer*. You do pause in the second sentence. Those words are set apart from the rest of the sentence. This changes the meaning of the sentence. While the first sentence says that the group that doesn't have a drummer was boring, the second sentence says that the group usually has a drummer and that it is boring without one.

Understand It

There are four main times to use a comma.

■ Use a comma to separate independent clauses connected with *and, but, or, not, for, so,* and *yet.*

> The skating instructor fell, and we had to pick him up.

■ Set off beginning elements in a sentence with a comma. These beginning elements include dependent clauses, prepositional phrases, and interjections.

> In the stadium, there is a skating rink. (**In the stadium** is a prepositional phrase.)

■ Use commas to separate the elements in a series.

> His roller skates are cracked, old, and ugly. (**Cracked, old, and ugly** are adjectives.)

> We skated till we were too tired to continue, slept for an hour, and skated again. (**Were too tired to continue, slept for an hour, and skated again** are phrases.)

 More About Commas Using too many commas can be just as confusing as using too few. To check your use of commas, say the sentence to yourself. Add a comma where you would take a short pause.

■ If a phrase or clause is essential to a sentence, do not use a comma. If the phrase or clause is not essential, use a comma.

> The boy **who does back flips** won the contest. (The phrase **who does back flips** is essential to the meaning of the sentence; the boy won because he does back flips.)
>
> The boy, **who does back flips,** won the contest. (The phrase in commas, **who does back flips**, is not essential to the meaning of the sentence. The fact that he won the contest did not depend on his ability to do back flips.)

▶ Add commas to the following sentences where appropriate.

1. We have oranges trail mix and sandwiches in our backpacks.

2. On top of this mountain and the other one there is a lodge.

3. Before I head down let me put on my goggles.

4. The instructor and his student skied down the bumpy slope.

Apply It

5. Edit the following passage, using this mark through commas you want to delete ✐ and this mark ⌄ for commas you want to add.

> During World War II a group of men who became known as the
>
> 10th Mountain Division, trained in the Colorado mountains.
>
> According, to the history books they learned to ski shoot and
>
> survive outdoors in freezing weather. Later, they were pioneers in
>
> the ski industry and helped, to make the sport popular.

Lesson 39   Semicolons

▪▪

If the period tells the reader to stop and the comma tells the reader to pause, the semicolon is something in between—a sort of weak period.

Define It

Like a comma, a **semicolon** groups parts of sentences. Semicolons, however, separate similar grammatical forms.

Understand It

Most often, semicolons are used to connect independent clauses. They can replace conjunctions such as *and*, *but*, and *for*.

> The guests are late; we don't know who is really coming. (The semicolon replaces the word **and**.)

You can also use semicolons in a list that has commas within the items.

> Meg looked for the captain of the volleyball team, a friend; the head of the student council, her cousin; and the spelling bee champion. (The semicolons show that the captain of the volleyball team is a friend and that the head of the student council is her cousin. Meg is looking for three people. Without the semicolons, she would be looking for five people.)

▶ On another sheet of paper, rewrite each sentence to use semicolons properly.

1. He made pasta, which was delicious, salad, which tasted like weeds, and dessert, which was a blueberry pie.

2. We came to dinner late, no one noticed.

3. Forget the wilted lettuce, and we will use tomatoes instead.

4. After the terrible meal, the only people left were the host, who was asleep, the waiter, who was cleaning up, and me.

Apply It

5. Find a piece of writing you have done, or select a newspaper story. Rewrite it on another sheet of paper, using semicolons where appropriate.

Lesson 40   Colons

Colons tell your reader that more information is on the way.

Define It

Colons direct attention to what is to follow.

Understand It

Here are some rules for using colons.

■ You can use a colon when an independent clause introduces a list.

> The rescue team consists of three people: a doctor, a diver, and a pilot. (The colon follows the noun **people**.)

■ Do not use a colon, however, immediately after a preposition or a verb. Either reword the sentence or omit the colon.

> The rescue team consists of a doctor, a diver, and a pilot. (A colon is not needed after the preposition **of** to introduce the list.)

■ Use a colon to separate two main clauses when the second describes or restates the first.

> The situation is dangerous: we must rescue the divers.

 More About Colons A colon introduces what is to follow; a semicolon separates grammatically similar forms.

1. Write in the appropriate punctuation in these sentences.

> The time has come we must dive. The equipment we need is an
>
> oxygen tank, a pair of pliers, and a set of hooks. We have rescued
>
> people in several states Florida, Maine, and New York.

Apply It

2. Write a short paragraph about a shopping trip you need to take. Be sure to include a sentence with two main clauses separated by a colon and another sentence with a colon that introduces a list.

Lesson 41 Apostrophes

....

Imagine that someone wrote you a note that said, "Go get the dogs food." What would you look for? An apostrophe in that sentence would tell you whether you should get enough food for one dog—or more.

Define It

Apostrophes are often used in two places: with **contractions** and with **possessives**. They are also used with some plurals.

Understand It

Here are the rules for using apostrophes correctly.

In contractions, apostrophes take the place of letters. *Do not* becomes *don't*. *Cannot* becomes *can't*. The apostrophes signal that letters are missing.

> He **shouldn't** have done that. (**Shouldn't** is the contraction of **should not**.)

Some plurals of letters, words, and abbreviations that use periods also take apostrophes.

> There are two **p's** in that word.
>
> There are five **many's** in that article.
>
> Two **M.D.'s** are in the waiting room.

The most frequent use of apostrophes, though, is to indicate possessive nouns—nouns that show that something belongs to someone or something. Here are the rules for forming possessive nouns with apostrophes.

- Singular nouns form the possessive by adding an apostrophe followed by -*s*.

> The **musician's** guitar was important to her.

- Most singular nouns that end in -*s* also add an apostrophe and -*s*:

> His **boss's** salary was high.

■ Plural nouns that do not end in -s form the possessive by adding an apostrophe and -s.

> The **children's** rooms were messy.

■ A plural noun that ends in -s ends with an apostrophe alone.

> Their **friends'** applause cheered up the runners.

 More About Apostrophes Don't add an apostrophe to possessive pronouns like *mine, yours, ours, its, theirs,* or *whose.* They already show ownership.

■ When you have a compound subject and you want to show that two people own one thing, add the apostrophe to the second subject. When you want to show that they own separate things, add the apostrophe to each subject.

> Jamie and **Sue's** project was due yesterday. (Jamie and Sue have one project.)
>
> **Jamie's** and **Sue's** projects were due yesterday. (Jamie and Sue have two separate projects.)

▶ Place apostrophes where necessary in the following sentences. Some sentences do not need apostrophes.

1. Many friends of theirs thought they would become police officers.

2. There are two ds and three ms in my fathers name.

3. Ours are stored next to Amy and Marks book.

4. Jonis bookshelves are filled with womens literature.

5. Theres nothing wrong with Megs and Lanss ideas, but whos supposed to make them happen?

6. Somebody elses dogs are on Lisas front porch.

Apply It

7. Write a short story. Use at least four of the following words: *Ross, crowd, shoes, Chris, dresses, Fred.* Also use the contractions for *cannot, will not, they are,* and *you will.*

Lesson 42   Quotation Marks

When you quote something, you state exactly what a person said. Quotes show another person's ideas and add excitement to writing.

Define It

Quotation marks go around the actual words someone has spoken or written, as in this example.

> "I wish I could buy whatever I wanted," Sheryl said.

Understand It

Here are the rules for using quotation marks.

- Use single quotation marks around quotations within quotations.

> "He told me, 'I am the richest man in the world,'" Brad said.

- In general, use a comma to separate a quotation from the rest of the sentence. Here are two examples of ways to quote a sentence. Notice that the quoted sentence in the second example begins with a capital letter because it also begins a sentence.

> "Find me the ring," George said.
>
> George said, "Find me the ring."

- Here is a divided sentence being quoted.

> "Find it for me," George said, "or I'll scream."

- Here is the punctuation for two sentences divided by an explanatory phrase.

> "Find it for me," George said. "I want the ring now."

- When the sentence ends with a question mark or an exclamation mark, use this form.

> "Find it for me!" George said.

- Place question marks and exclamation points that are not part of the quote outside the quotation marks.

> "Did you say, 'Find it for me'?" Mary asked.
>
> Did he really say, "I want to do the dance alone"?

 More About Quotations Start a new paragraph whenever a new speaker begins speaking.

▶ Add quotation marks and punctuation where they are needed in the following sentences. If a letter needs to be capitalized, underline it three times. (Three lines under a letter or word is an editing mark that means that the letter or word should be capitalized.) Use these marks to add quotation marks: ⸜, ⸝, ˅, and ˅.

1. Jamie said come with me! They're after us!

2. Raul said to me I'd like to borrow your science notes Then we started

talking Gale said.

3. Oh, no They are both gone Jack exclaimed Now what are we going

to do

4. Wallis answered nothing. There is nothing we can do.

5. By the time I got there Cyndra said everyone was already celebrating

Apply It

6. On a separate sheet of paper, write a dialogue between two people caught in an exciting situation. For example, they could be skydiving, rafting, or running away from a forest fire.

Lesson 43   Dashes and Parentheses

Dashes and parentheses—which you've probably seen in magazine or newspaper articles—are used in similar ways. They break up sentences and add extra information for the reader.

Define It

Use **dashes** to show a sharp turn in the thought of a sentence or to enclose explanations or examples. Like colons, they can also introduce a list.

> We thought—but you knew this—that the painting was a forgery. (The dashes show a sharp turn in thought.)
>
> The other painting—that one over there—is the real masterpiece. (The dashes enclose an explanation.)
>
> Those were the paintings—a van Gogh, a Cassatt, and a Monet. (The dash introduces a list.)

Parentheses also can give the reader additional information. While dashes emphasize information, parentheses minimize its importance.

> I told Jack—you do know Jack, I believe—to put back the crown. (The dashes make the clause **you do know Jack, I believe** seem like an important part of the sentence.)
>
> I told Jack (you do know Jack, I believe) to put back the crown. (The parentheses make the clause **you do know Jack, I believe** seem less important.)

Two of the other uses of parentheses are to enclose an acronym (the initials of an organization) after you have written its name out and to include information that's not a necessary part of the sentence.

> The Center for Our Energy (**COE**) is involved with that. (**COE** is an acronym.)
>
> They told Jack (his name was once Phil) not to come back. (The information **his name was once Phil** is not a necessary part of the sentence.)

More About Punctuation You can use several kinds of punctuation for the same task, such as adding information. The best writing uses a variety of punctuation and doesn't overdo any one kind.

Understand It

▶ Rewrite the following sentences on the lines below. Include the phrase in italics somewhere in the sentence, but punctuate it with either a dash (or dashes) or with parentheses.

1. *as you are aware* This joking around must stop immediately.

_____

2. *once called Fun World* Fun Park is on the other side of town.

_____

3. *pictures of children, of flowers, and of love* The photographs stirred deep feelings in us all.

_____

4. *correct me if I am wrong* I am convinced that you are not telling the truth.

_____

5. *an orange, a banana, and an apricot* We ate all the fruit.

_____

Apply It

6. On the lines below, write a paragraph about a spying mission. In your paragraph, include dashes and items in parentheses.

_____

_____

_____

_____

_____

_____

_____

Lesson 44   Hyphens

You probably know hyphens as the marks at the ends of lines that show that a word is continued on the next line. Hyphens have more jobs than that, though.

Define It

A **hyphen** can divide words that are too long to fit at the end of a line. When you divide words into syllables, make sure the second line has at least three letters of the word. For example, do not hyphenate *pointed* as *point-ed*. When you are in doubt about how to divide a word into syllables, check a dictionary.

In addition, a hyphen can join two or more words to make a single adjective or a compound word.

He stared at the **ice-covered** sidewalk. (**Ice** and **covered** are joined to make one adjective.)

My **great-grandmother** is coming to visit. (**Great** and **grandmother** are joined to make a compound word.)

A hyphen also joins compound numbers from twenty-one through ninety-nine.

Fifty-five band members left the stage.

Understand It

▶ Imagine the following words are at the ends of lines. Rewrite them to show possible hyphenation (*re-spon-si-ble*, for example).

1. pleasant   _____

2. chocolate   _____

3. forgetfulness   _____

4. vitamins   _____

Apply It

5. On another sheet of paper, write a description of the sunset, using at least two hyphenated adjectives. Also hyphenate at least two words that will not fit at the end of a line.

Lesson 45　Titles

Do you know when to underline, italicize, and use quotations for the titles of movies, books, and articles? Here is a short overview.

Define It

Titles of books, plays, articles, and poems, are punctuated in different ways.

Capitalize all words except short prepositions and articles in book titles, plays, magazines, newspapers, television shows, and long musical works. All these words should be italicized as well. If you are using a typewriter or are hand-writing your work, you can underline instead of italicizing. See the examples below for the use of italics and underlining. The use of capital letters is the same in both cases.

> *A Tale of Two Cities* is a good book. (Use italics when working on a computer.)
>
> <u>A Tale of Two Cities</u> is a good book. (Use underlining when not working on a computer.)

Put quotation marks around the titles of short stories, essays, short poems, songs, episodes of television shows, and articles in magazines and newspapers. Capitalize all words except short prepositions and articles.

> When you read his short story "The Pretzel," you will know where the idea for her song "The Pretzel Rush" comes from.

Understand It

1. Underline and use quotation marks where appropriate in the following sentences. Draw three lines under letters that should be capitalized.

> Sidney's book, the time to come, is based on a short story,
>
> another time, which appeared in the magazine Tomorrow. Sidney
>
> even has plans to make it into a play called always another time.

Apply It

2. On another sheet of paper, write a one-paragraph review of a short story, a newspaper article, a song, a book, or a play. Exchange papers with another student and check for correct use of capitalization and punctuation.

Lesson 46   Numbers

You often need to use numbers in your writing. But writing numbers can cause writers to pause: should the numbers be written in words or in numerals?

Define It

Numbers of one hundred or fewer and all numbers rounded to hundreds are usually spelled out. If a number begins a sentence, it is always spelled out.

> Mozart was **sixteen** when he composed some of his music.
>
> About **twelve hundred** people were in the audience.
>
> The school had **384** students enrolled in it.
>
> **Three hundred eighty-four** students were enrolled in the school.

 TIP

More About Numbers There is no *and* between the word *hundred* and whichever two-digit number follows it. Thus, you would say "two hundred ten," not "two hundred *and* ten."

Add a comma in numbers that have four or more places. Count from the right and use a comma after every three places.

1,342	239,132	45,691,013
32,696	1,945,612	552,771,005

Understand It

▶ Rewrite these sentences on another sheet of paper so they are correct. Some sentences may already be correct.

1. 1,000 students decided to study music in 1980, but only 657 graduated, and of those, only 400 got jobs.

2. Of the fifteen people in the class, four were ready to go.

3. 345 different instruments are on display; of those, 90 are violins, 13 are drums, and 59 are trumpets.

Apply It

4. On a separate sheet of paper, write a paragraph that describes how you solved a math problem. Begin at least one sentence with a number.

1. The following paragraphs contain errors using mechanics. On another sheet of paper, rewrite the paragraphs so these errors are eliminated.

"Wow." Did mary tell you what we saw last night. Heather asked.

"No." David said. Maybe you, could fill, us in."

Well; it started when Jack, Pete and I went to that restaurant last night? It's called the yellow hen. Heather said, We saw senator Millings you know, the senator against school funding. He's a friend of my great aunt."

"What happened next?" David asked.

"Jack went right up to him and this is what he said! Heather told David. Senator, have you seen our school. Do you know what shape its in. Let me tell you how bad it is the ceilings are leaking 6 doors are gone and the floors are ripped up. What are you going to do about it. That's what he said.

"What did the Senator do," David asked.

"He said he would have a group of 14 people look into it, I don't know who they would be, and put his administrative aide in charge Heather said.

2. On another sheet of paper, write a short story about two people who want to change a situation in the world or in their lives. In your story, use as many types of punctuation as you can. When you revise, pay careful attention to your use of mechanics.

UNIT 2 Editor's Checklist

Editing your work is an important step in the writing process. After you have completed your first draft, use this checklist to make sure that your work is clear and that it says what you want to say.

Use this checklist to help you assess the way you build sentences.

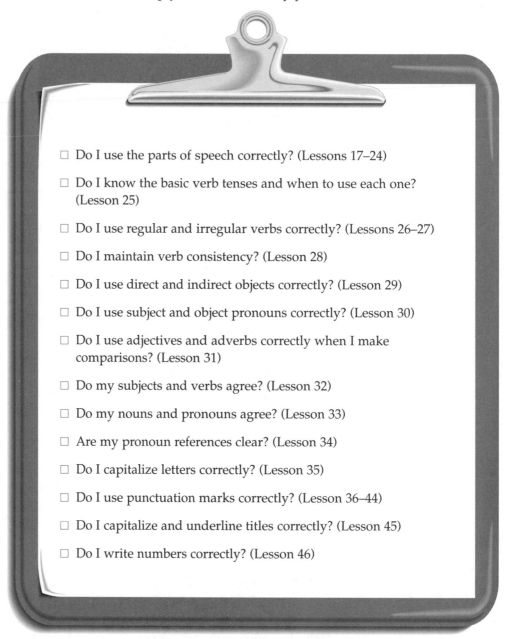

☐ Do I use the parts of speech correctly? (Lessons 17–24)

☐ Do I know the basic verb tenses and when to use each one? (Lesson 25)

☐ Do I use regular and irregular verbs correctly? (Lessons 26–27)

☐ Do I maintain verb consistency? (Lesson 28)

☐ Do I use direct and indirect objects correctly? (Lesson 29)

☐ Do I use subject and object pronouns correctly? (Lesson 30)

☐ Do I use adjectives and adverbs correctly when I make comparisons? (Lesson 31)

☐ Do my subjects and verbs agree? (Lesson 32)

☐ Do my nouns and pronouns agree? (Lesson 33)

☐ Are my pronoun references clear? (Lesson 34)

☐ Do I capitalize letters correctly? (Lesson 35)

☐ Do I use punctuation marks correctly? (Lesson 36–44)

☐ Do I capitalize and underline titles correctly? (Lesson 45)

☐ Do I write numbers correctly? (Lesson 46)

UNIT 2 What Have You Learned?

Multiple Choice

In each blank, write the letter of the word or words that best completes each sentence.

1. _____ I (a) seen (b) saw (c) sees (d) sawed Peter come in.

2. _____ (a) Him and I (b) He and I (c) Them and I (d) Her and I gave them the keys.

3. _____ Patti is the (a) young (b) most young (c) youngest (d) younger of the two sisters.

4. _____ Ed slept while I (a) climbs (b) climbed (c) climb (d) did climb the stairs.

5. _____ The actress and her friends (a) dance (b) dances (c) dancing (d) has dances through the door.

6. _____ Did you see that tiger (a)? (b) . (c) ! (d) ; It jumped the fence.

7. _____ Junik's (a) friend's (b) friends (c) friends' (d) friends's are with her.

8. _____ The crowd waited for (a) President Clinton. (b) president clinton. (c) president Clinton. (d) the President.

Fill in the Blanks

There are some grammatical problems in the following sentences. Circle the error and write the correct usage in the blank. If there are no errors, write *none*.

9. _____ Jeremy and Rose knew that their's was the right answer.

10. _____ Why don't you and Jenny leave that baby alone.

11. _____ Wait a minute; let's look at that paper again.

12. _____ She and Sammy goes to the store, but they always come back.

13. _____ If Darcey and me were still friends, I'd take him to the movie.

UNIT 3   Analyzing Sentence Style

As you've read in this book, it's easier to read—and understand—writing that uses different kinds and different lengths of sentences. Learning to revise your writing for clarity and interest is the final step to developing a clear, interesting writing style.

Define It

Sentence style is knowing how to write sentences so they don't sound alike. It is also knowing how to combine sentences and to use different sentence beginnings to engage your reader. Just as important is learning how to construct paragraphs. Finally, every writer should know the final step to any writing process: checking your work and revising to make sure your message comes through to your reader.

Understand It

How much do you already know about sentence style? Read these paragraphs. The first is a more effective paragraph. Can you tell why?

Example A

Sometimes the best intentions turn sour. In the 1890s, a man who loved Shakespeare decided to bring to the United States every bird mentioned in Shakespeare's plays. One of those birds, the grackle, is now one of the biggest pests in this country.

Example B

In the 1890s a man who loved Shakespeare made a decision. It was decided by him to bring to the United States some birds. He decided to bring every bird mentioned in Shakespeare's plays. The best intentions turn sour. One of those birds was the grackle. The grackle is now one of the biggest pests in this country.

Apply It

1. Use what you know about sentences to discuss Examples A and B with a classmate. Discuss why Example A is a more effective paragraph than Example B.

2. Fill out the first two columns in the chart below with what you know and what you want to know about sentence style. At the end of the unit, fill out the third column.

What I Know	What I Want to Know	What I Learned

CHAPTER 7   Varying Sentences

This chapter is about style—sentence style. By varying the kinds of sentences you write, your writing will be more interesting to read—and to write.

Define It

Varying sentences means making sure that not every sentence you write looks or sounds the same. One way to vary sentences is to learn to use the active and passive voices. You can also vary your sentences by combining short sentences, by using different ways to begin sentences, and by using transitions.

Understand It

1. What do you already know about varying sentences? On the lines below, revise this paragraph to make it more interesting to read.

> Hernando de Soto was a gold seeker. He was one of the most famous of all time. It was thought by him that there was gold in Florida. He went there. He was feared by his men, who only stayed because they were told by de Soto that they would become rich. De Soto knew his men would not stay with him if he did not tell them that. De Soto drove his men hard. He told them that gold was just ahead. He fell ill and died near the Mississippi River. He found no gold.

_____

_____

_____

_____

_____

_____

_____

_____

Apply It

2. Discuss your revision with a classmate. Discuss why you made the changes you did and how they improved the way the paragraph sounds.

Lesson 47 Combining Sentences

Short sentences make an impact. But if you use only short sentences, your writing will not flow. Your reader also may have a hard time telling which of your ideas are related to one another.

Define It

When you **combine sentences**, you put several short sentences together so that the new sentence contains related ideas. Combining sentences helps make writing smoother and gives it more variety and interest. Look at the difference between these two examples.

> We left the island the next morning. The sun was shining.
>
> *Combined sentences*: The sun was shining when we left the island the next morning. (The sun was shining at the same time as they left the island.)

Understand It

There are several ways to combine sentences.

- One is to create **compound sentences**.

> The island was far away. It took days to get there.
>
> The island was far away, **and** it took days to get there. (The coordinating conjunction **and** and a comma combine the sentences.)

- You can also use a semicolon and an adverb to combine sentences, or you can use a semicolon alone.

> The island was far away; **therefore,** it took days to get there.
>
> The island was far away; it took days to get there.

- Another way to combine sentences is to turn one of the sentences into a dependent clause.

> **Because the island was far away,** it took days to get there.

■ A phrase can also combine sentences.

> I looked at the island. It was glimmering in the moonlight.
>
> I looked at the island **glimmering in the moonlight.**

■ Finally, you can combine sentences by rewriting the sentences to join their details.

> I saw flowers on the island. They were red.
>
> I saw **red flowers** on the island.

1. Rewrite this paragraph on the lines below. Use different techniques for combining sentences for smoothness and clarity.

> I will never forget the island. I loved it. I remember the sand. It was white. It sparkled in the sun. The time came to go. I hid in the bushes. The bushes hid me well. No one could find me. I finally came out. I got on the ship. I said farewell to the island.

_____

_____

_____

_____

_____

_____

Apply It

2. Find two or more paragraphs of your writing. Use what you learned in this lesson about combining sentences to revise your writing so that it sounds smoother and more varied.

Lesson 48   Transition Words

Think of transition words as guides through your writing. They can show readers how your ideas relate to one another and what's coming next.

Define It

Transition words show the relationship between ideas in sentences and between ideas in paragraphs.

Understand It

Here are some transition words that can be useful.

To show time: *later, soon, then, next, at the same time*

To add information: *in addition, besides, also, too, next*

To compare: *similarly, likewise*

To contrast: *but, yet, on the other hand, however*

To show examples: *one, another, for example, for instance*

To show results: *as a result, consequently, therefore, thus*

More About Transition Words It's probably easiest to look for transitions when you're revising. Add transition words where you seem to shift ideas too quickly.

Apply It

1. Copy the passage below. Fill in each blank with one of these transitions: *for example, also, finally, however.*

Working as a camp counselor can be a great way to spend the

summer. _____, you should know what both you and the camp

expect. _____, think about your salary. _____ make sure you

understand the rules of the camp. _____, remember to have fun.

2. Underline the transition words you used in an essay you have written. Does each one help to guide your reader through your work? Rewrite the essay, if necessary, to include more effective transition words.

Lesson 49   Active and Passive Voice

Compare the following two descriptions of a game that was decided in the last second. Example A: *The pass was thrown by the quarterback to the tight end. The game was won by West Side.* Example B: *The quarterback threw the pass to the tight end. West Side won the game.* The second version is more exciting because it is written in the active voice.

Define It

In the **active voice**, the subject performs the action. Use the active voice to create excitement and to draw a clear picture. Here is an example.

Doris painted a mural for the auditorium.

In the **passive voice**, the past participle of the main verb is added to a form of the verb *to be*. Use the passive voice when you don't know the performer of the action or when the performer isn't important. In most cases, avoid the passive voice.

A mural for the auditorium **was painted by** Doris.
(Doris does not seem to be responsible for the painting.)

 More About Active and Passive Voice To change passive voice to active voice, revise the sentence so that the person or thing that performs the action is the subject of the sentence.

Understand It

1. On another sheet of paper, revise this paragraph, changing the passive voice to the active voice when appropriate.

   The vegetables were picked by Lamy. Then they were cooked by the school chef. By the time they were served, though, the vegetables had turned to mush. It was thought by Jim that the food cooked by the chef was terrible. It was thought by him that a petition drive should be started by someone to get a new chef.

Apply It

2. Look through a book, newspaper, or magazine and find three examples of the passive voice. Copy these sentences onto another sheet of paper. Then rewrite each sentence, changing each one to active voice. Finally, compare the sentences. How does the revision to active voice change the sound of each sentence?

Lesson 50   Varying Sentence Beginnings

I tiptoed to the door. I listened for another thud. I could hear nothing. I thought I'd been mistaken. I heard it again. This should be an exciting scene, but it's not. Why? Every sentence begins in the same way, with the pronoun *I.*

Define It

By **varying sentence beginnings**, you can add interest to your writing.

Understand It

Here are some possibilities.

- Begin a sentence with one or more adjectives:

> **Black and fuzzy,** pandas appeal to everyone.

- Begin a sentence with a dependent clause.

> **When it finished the plants,** the giraffe munched the trees.

- Begin a sentence with a phrase.

> **Humming softly to herself,** the trainer tossed the food into the cage.

- Begin a sentence with a prepositional phrase.

> **In a minute,** the monkeys will yawn.

- Begin a sentence with a noun.

> **A crowd pleaser,** Lucy the elephant had many fans.

More About Sentence Beginnings Remember that not every phrase, adverb, or adverb clause can be moved to the beginning of a sentence. Sometimes, shifting words causes a misplaced modifier, as in *Flying over the tree, Carrie saw the eagle.*

▶ Rewrite the following sentences, using one of the types of sentence beginnings on page 92.

1. The macaws flew around the cage, squawking when they saw anyone approach.

_____

_____

2. The trainer, a normally cheerful man, was saddened by the death of the gibbon.

_____

_____

3. The gibbon, unfortunately, had been his favorite ape.

_____

_____

4. The cool, collected veterinarian didn't hesitate before he put his hand in the lion's mouth.

_____

_____

5. The monkeys will be let out of their cages in a few minutes, if they stop jabbering.

_____

_____

6. The attendant held the doors of the zoo open so that the last visitors could leave, smiling all the while.

_____

_____

Apply It

7. On another sheet of paper, write a few paragraphs that describe the plot of a television show or a movie you enjoyed. When you revise, be sure that you use a variety of sentence beginnings.

1. Use the techniques you learned in this chapter to revise the paragraphs below. Combine sentences to make them clearer and more varied, add transition words to guide your reader, use the active voice when appropriate, and vary the sentence beginnings.

The sport of hiking is done by many people, for many reasons. They like to move their legs, to get exercise, and to see beautiful places.

There are so many reasons to hike they can't all be named by me.

I can tell you why I hike. I hike, smelling the flowers and breathing the fresh air. I hike to get a different view of the world for a few hours. I am happy and at peace before long. I know that the good effects will be felt by me for a long time afterward.

_____

_____

_____

_____

_____

_____

2. On another sheet of paper, write an essay about an outdoor activity you enjoy. Use the techniques you learned in this chapter to revise your writing so that it flows smoothly and is exciting to read.

CHAPTER 8   Building Paragraphs

Paragraphs are one way to organize your writing. You use them to group your ideas and to help guide your reader through the information you want to give them.

Define It

When you build paragraphs, you fit ideas together. To do this, you need to know what point you want to make in your paragraph, how to support your point, and how to organize the information within the paragraph.

Understand It

1. How much do you know about paragraphs? Reorder the sentences in this paragraph so a reader can easily understand its point.

> The color of the product isn't always the same as what you saw in the catalog. If you're careful and know about these problems, though, you might find that mail-order buying is a good idea for you. Some catalog companies make returning what you buy difficult. Although many people like to buy from mail-order catalogs, there are some problems with doing this. You don't get what you buy right away.

_____

_____

_____

_____

_____

_____

_____

_____

Apply It

2. Discuss your revision with a classmate. Did you make the same changes? Discuss why you revised the paragraph the way you did. Then work together to revise the paragraph so you both are satisfied with it.

Lesson 51   The Paragraph

If words are the building blocks of a sentence, sentences are the material you use to build a paragraph.

Define It

A **paragraph** develops an idea or a topic. Many of the paragraphs you write will state the idea at the beginning, then back up that idea with reasons. By the end of the paragraph, your reader will know why you think as you do.

Understand It

Not all paragraphs are alike. In fact, they shouldn't be. Sometimes a writer will use a single sentence as a paragraph. That technique draws attention to the paragraph. Other paragraphs walk a reader through an argument.

One thing that paragraphs have in common is the way they look. In most writing, the first line of each paragraph is indented. In some writing, however, a blank line separates two paragraphs.

 More About Paragraphs If you can't decide how to divide your paragraphs, list your main ideas. Each main idea and the sentences that support or explain it should be in a separate paragraph.

Apply It

1. On another sheet of paper, revise this writing to form three clear paragraphs.

Should you buy a car? There are some good reasons to consider it. One reason is that you can go where you want when you want to go. Another reason is that the sense of freedom you get from having your own car is thrilling. There are good reasons, though, to think twice about buying a car. Cars can be very expensive. They can become a magnet for friends who want to borrow them, which means you have to learn to say no to your friends. What you have to do is weigh the pros and cons. On the one hand, you have freedom and the knowledge that you don't have to rely on buses or friends for a ride. On the other hand, you have the great expense and worry of having a car. Only you know if buying a car makes sense for you.

2. On another sheet of paper, write an argument about why teenagers should be allowed to do something, such as stay out later on weekends. Make sure each paragraph you write develops only one idea.

Lesson 52   Topic Sentences

Reading a paragraph without a topic sentence is like trying to find your way in a new city without a map. Having a main idea in your mind as you write helps you plan an effective paragraph.

Define It

The main idea of a paragraph is the paragraph's purpose. It is the point you want to make. This idea is often expressed in a **topic sentence**.

Understand It

Constructing an effective topic sentence takes care. A topic sentence that is too broad is difficult to cover in a paragraph. *The wolf is an interesting animal* is an example of a topic sentence that is too broad. Here is an example of an effective topic sentence.

> Returning the wolf to the wild has little support among old-timers in the West.

A topic sentence that is too narrow can also cause problems. If the topic sentence discusses how wolves *used to* attack cattle, the rest of the paragraph should not address how ranchers feel *today* about wolves.

Most often, a topic sentence is the first sentence in a paragraph. This method of organization can help your readers understand your ideas. As they read the rest of the paragraph, they see the sentences that support the topic sentence. (This paragraph has its topic sentence first. The rest of the sentences in the paragraph then support this topic sentence.)

More About Topic Sentences If your paragraph seems to wander, think about the main point you want to make. Write a new topic sentence and arrange your arguments so that they support it. Sentences that don't fit in your new paragraph may work well in another paragraph.

Apply It

▶ On a separate sheet of paper, write a possible topic sentence based on each of the broad topics listed below.

1. Television ratings

2. Computer use by students

3. Sports

Lesson 53   Supporting Sentences

Think of a paragraph as a chair. While the seat is the topic sentence, the legs are the supporting sentences. Without them, the chair would collapse.

Define It

The **supporting sentences** in a paragraph give the details that explain the topic sentence. While the kind of supporting details varies, writers often use stories, facts, examples, and reasons in their supporting sentences.

More About Supporting Sentences Every sentence in a paragraph should support the topic sentence. If a sentence doesn't support the main idea, either move it to another paragraph or rewrite it.

Understand It

It's probably best to use only one type of supporting sentence in each paragraph. If you use several types, your paragraph may sound confused.

Here are examples of the different kinds of supporting sentences. They all could be used to support this topic sentence.

> *Topic sentence:* Returning the wolf to the wild has little support among old-timers in the West.

- **Stories** can create a vivid picture in the reader's mind and make writing interesting to read.

> One diary entry of a Montana rancher from the 1800s describes how a wolf pack surrounded a cow and her calf and attacked them. (This is a story that supports the topic sentence.)

- **Facts** are statements you can prove. They may be statistics, historical information, or information that everyone knows to be true.

> For generations, ranchers and farmers shot wolves whenever they saw them. (It is a fact that early ranchers shot wolves when they saw them.)

- **Examples** help make a larger idea understandable. An example can illustrate a paragraph's main idea.

> One wolf could easily kill a sheep or cow and cause the others to stampede. (This is just one example of the damage wolves could do to a rancher's livestock.)

- **Reasons** are statements that explain or give more information to show that a topic sentence is correct. Writers often use reasons when they are writing to persuade.

> For these ranchers, who grew up with horror stories of wolves, the idea of trying to bring these animals back is hard to understand. (This is one reason ranchers do not support the return of the wolf to the West.)

1. Choose a magazine article that interests you. Find one paragraph in it that includes a topic sentence and supporting statements. On the lines below, write the topic sentence and label it. Then write the supporting sentences, identifying each as a story, a fact, an example, or a reason.

_____

_____

_____

_____

_____

_____

_____

_____

Apply It

2. Think of an issue that interests you. You might like to write about why movie tickets should cost less or why your school needs a new gym. On another sheet of paper, write a topic sentence for a paragraph on this topic. Follow it with supporting sentences that explain and support the topic sentence.

Lesson 54 Organizing Paragraphs

The order in which sentences appear is as important as the information they contain. You must arrange information logically so your reader can understand your ideas.

Define It

When you **organize paragraphs**, you decide on the structure of each paragraph. An effective organizational plan will help your readers understand the purpose of every paragraph you write.

More About Organizing Paragraphs It's easiest to choose an organizational plan before you begin writing. Think about how you might explain your ideas to someone else. Then use that plan when you write.

Understand It

Here are several ways to organize paragraphs.

■ You can organize a paragraph in **chronological order**, or time order, by presenting events in the order in which they happened. This plan works best when you are describing a historical event, telling a story, or explaining the steps needed to do something.

> Anyone can make an omelet. To start, heat the pan and melt a little butter in it. Then whip the eggs and pour them carefully into the hot pan. Next, wait until the edges of the omelet are cooked. Now add the filling on half of the omelet and carefully flip the other half over. After a few seconds, the omelet will be done.

■ You can write a paragraph in **spatial order**. Writers often use this plan when they want to describe a scene from one side to the other.

> There were flowers everywhere. On one side of the hill, lilacs bloomed. Next to them, a cherry tree dripped with blossoms. Opposite the lilacs was a field of tulips, their colorful heads waving in the wind.

■ You can also organize your ideas by their **order of importance**. You can begin a paragraph with the least important fact or story, then build with more important facts. This plan builds reader interest and leaves a strong impression. You can also begin with the most important supporting fact or story to immediately grab your reader's interest.

> I need a new bike. The handlebars and the frame are rusty. The front wheel is bent. Worst of all, though, is that the brakes don't work when I'm going downhill.

■ You can use **classification** by creating categories within a paragraph. For example, you might write that there are intramural sports in your school, and then use a sentence to describe each one.

> My school has three intramural teams that are successful this year. The tennis team is undefeated in the city league. The baseball team has lost only one game. Finally, the soccer team has won four out of six games this season.

■ You can **compare**, or show how items are alike, in a paragraph. You can also **contrast** items, or show how they are different.

> Baseball is not as destructive as football. First, football players are praised for their huge size and ability to hurt, while size matters less in baseball. Second, football players are supposed to run into each other. In baseball no one has the job of running into someone else.

■ You can organize a paragraph by **cause and effect**. You do this to show relationships—why one event caused another.

> Why did the students walk out? If you ask them, they will say that the reason was simple. They walked out because they did not feel that they were involved in the planning of the drop-in center.

1. Find a paragraph in a newspaper or in a textbook that follows one of the forms of organization discussed in this lesson. Copy it on a separate sheet of paper and label the organizing plan the writer used.

Apply It

2. On a separate sheet of paper, write two paragraphs that are organized in different ways. They may be on different topics or on the same topic. Label each paragraph with the organizing plan you used.

1. Read the following short report. The report has errors in the topic sentences, the supporting sentences, and paragraph organization. On another sheet of paper, revise the report so that it reads smoothly and the writer's ideas are clear.

Chocolate is made from the seeds of the cacao tree. Chocolate is very popular with almost everyone. The seeds grow inside pods on the trees. Then the seeds, or beans, are taken from the pod.

The beans go into huge machines. When they arrive at the factory, the beans are roasted, which brings out their taste. Then they are ground until they form a dark brown liquid. From there, the chocolate is made into bars and cocoa.

When Hernán Cortés came to Mexico, he tasted the drink flavored with cinnamon, sugar, and vanilla, and he loved it. Chocolate has long been used as a beverage. That was its first use, in fact. He later brought hot chocolate to Europe, and the drink became popular among the upper classes. Chocolate in the United States is very popular in bar form. Americans have a love affair with the tropical bean. The United States uses one-fourth of the world's production of cocoa beans in its factories.

2. Find a report you have written recently. Think about what you learned in this chapter about paragraph structure. Revise your report to improve your topic sentences, supporting sentences, and paragraph organization.

CHAPTER 9   Revising and Editing Your Work

Revising your work is as important as writing it. Careful revisions can help you make sure that your points are clear and that your reader can understand your ideas. Revising can also help you polish your choice of words so that you say exactly what you want to say.

Define It

Reading your work slowly to yourself or reading it aloud will help you find places where your thoughts or your wording are unclear. When you look at your writing with an editor's eye, you consider how well you have expressed your ideas and how well your writing holds together. Most writers move, revise, add, and subtract words and sentences to make their writing more effective.

In addition to making sure your ideas are clear, editing involves checking for mechanical errors. Mechanical errors—in grammar, word usage, punctuation, and spelling—can keep your reader from understanding what you want to say.

Understand It

1. Test your editing and revising skills. On another sheet of paper, revise these paragraphs to eliminate mechanical errors and to make the writing clearer.

> Fireworks were inventd in china in the tenth centry. Historians think a cook might have mixd together some pickling saltes, coal, and sulfer to make a fire. I have seen my mother use pickling salt to make pikles. The poor cook found his food explodeing. Their were few cookes who tryed that trick again.
>
> Then the chinese tryed the mixure not as a cooking feul, but as a roket. They used these rockts, also caled fireworks, to celebrate holidais and wedings. The chinese caled there fireworks "arrows of flyeing fire."

Apply It

2. With a classmate, discuss the changes you made. If your changes differ, discuss why you each made the revisions you did. Then rewrite the paragraphs on another sheet of paper, making the changes you both agree should be made.

Lesson 55   Unity

I think we should be able to have lunch outside. We can be trusted to come back to school on time. Reggie's Diner serves great lunches. We should try it for a week. What is this paragraph about?

Define It

A paragraph has **unity** when all of the supporting sentences are directly related to the topic sentence of the paragraph. As you revise your work, unity should be one of your main concerns.

Understand It

To be sure your paragraph has unity, reread the sentences you have written. Do they all directly support your topic sentence? If not, revise your writing so that your reader can be sure of your point.

If your paragraph has sentences that do not support the topic sentence, you have two choices. You might decide to delete these sentences. You might decide, though, that your supporting sentences are leading you to a different topic sentence. In that case, revise your topic sentence.

In any check for unity within a paragraph, look for the following things.

■ *A precise topic.* Do all the sentences in your paragraph support the topic sentence? If not, rewrite until all the sentences work together.

■ *Details that make your points.* If your evidence is not convincing, add supporting sentences that give more details about your topic.

■ *Smoothly linked sentences.* Check for sentences that seem to be out of place. These sentences will sound like you've changed direction.

Apply It

1. Rewrite the following paragraph so that it is unified. Be sure the supporting sentences make a case for the topic sentence.

> You have to give up some of your independence when you get a job. You sometimes have to cancel plans because you have to work. You may have to wear a uniform that's embarrassing. It's nice having extra money. Having a job can be a pain.

2. Choose a paragraph that you have written. On another sheet of paper, rewrite the paragraph, making sure that all of the sentences support your topic sentence. Then exchange papers with another student and edit each other's work for unity.

Lesson 56   Coherence

Coherence also helps to hold writing together. When a paragraph has coherence, all its ideas are connected in a way that makes sense.

Define It

When you revise for **coherence**, you make sure that your ideas are arranged in a logical order. You also check that they flow from one to another. Coherence concerns both the smooth flow of ideas and the appropriate choice of words.

Understand It

Here are some strategies for revising to make sure your writing is coherent.

- *Introduce your topic clearly.* If your reader reaches the end of your paragraph and isn't sure what you are talking about, you have a coherence problem. Be sure that your topic sentence reflects the main point of the paragraph.

- *Introduce unfamiliar ideas so that your reader can follow your argument.* To explain your points, you may need to use a technical term or describe a geographical location. Remember, one point of writing is to tell people things they don't know. If you are introducing ideas and words, explain them when you first mention them.

- *Plan how you will present your points.* You need to present your ideas in a way that your reader will understand. In some cases, using chronological order or order of importance makes sense. In other cases, another organizational plan would be a better choice. Use a plan that fits what you want to say.

- *Do what you promise to do in your topic sentence.* If you say you will discuss why people should buy a certain computer, don't talk about a different computer. If you say you will list three reasons, list three reasons—in the order you use in your topic sentence.

- *Be sure your transitions smoothly connect your ideas.* Transitions make your writing flow. They act as signposts that show your reader the way from one idea to the next.

 More About Coherence Words like *in addition, however, of course,* and *finally* help your reader move smoothly from one idea to the next.

1. On another sheet of paper, revise the following paragraph for coherence.

> Lutra canadensis is also a member of the weasel family. It lives in most of the United States and Canada. Trapping has killed many river otters. You may be surprised to hear how many animals are in the weasel family; here are three examples. The honey badger, or Mellivora capensis, is a member of the weasel family. It lives in Africa and the Middle East. Its skin is so tough it can tear into beehives and not get hurt. My brother once got near a beehive and was sick for days with the stings. The M. vision is also a weasel. This animal is also called a mink.

Apply It

▶ Find a paragraph you have written. Use the following questions to evaluate the paragraph. On the blanks, write specific sentences that work well and those that could be revised.

2. Did I introduce my topic clearly? _____ Example: _____

_____

3. Did I introduce unfamiliar ideas so my reader could follow my

argument? _____ Example: _____

_____

4. What plan did I use to present my points? _____ Example: _____

_____

_____

5. Did I do what I promised in my topic sentence? _____

Example: _____

_____

6. Do my transitions smoothly connect my ideas? _____

Example: _____

_____

Lesson 57 Editing Marks

Crossing out words and writing in changes is a type of shorthand that allows you to make notes that you'll use in your revision.

Define It   Writers and editors use **editing marks** to show where they want to revise.

Understand It   In the example below, an editor has made changes to improve a draft.

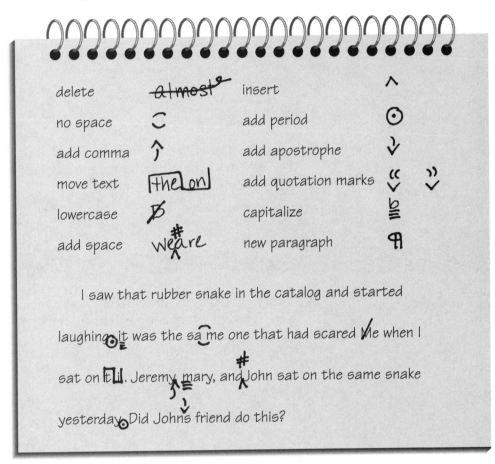

1. Use editing marks to revise the following paragraph.

> Like many inventions, the craetion Floating Soap was a mis-take the mixer was left on to long. When the soap finished, it had air whipped int o it. Peopleloved the new soap because they could find it in there bath tubs when they were takeing a bath.

Apply It   **2.** Choose a recent writing assignment and exchange papers with a classmate. Use editing marks to revise each other's work.

Lesson 58   Easily Confused Words

There are several sets of words that cause many writers to pause. Is it *there* or *they're*—or maybe *their*?

Define It

Here are some of the most commonly confused sets of words.

- *Bad, badly.* Use *bad* after linking words such as *feel*, *look*, and *seem*. Use *badly* as an adverb.

> He felt bad about not finishing.
>
> He performed badly on the typing test.

- *Can, may.* The verb *can* generally refers to the ability to do something; the verb *may* generally refers to permission to do something.

> Can you lift this 50-pound bag for me?
>
> May I walk to the cafeteria with you?

- *Good, well.* Use *good* after linking verbs such as *is, taste, feel, look,* and *seem.* Use *well* when you need an adverb.

> The ice cream tastes good.
>
> We knew the street well.

- *Its, it's. Its* is a possessive pronoun. *It's* is a contraction of "it is."

> The dog has something in its paw.
>
> It's time to leave.

More About Its and It's If you're not sure which form to use, change the contraction to the words *it is* and see if it makes sense in the sentence.

- *Lie, lay.* To *lie* is "to rest"; to *lay* is "to put something down." Remember that when you use the word *lay*, you need to lay an object down. The forms of the verb *lie* are *lie*, *lay*, *lain*, and *lying*. The forms of the verb *lay* are *lay*, *laid*, *laid*, and *laying*. The confusion with *lie* and *lay* arises because the past tense of *lie* is *lay*.

> I want to lie down and take a nap.
>
> I lay the pan on the stove before I turn on the heat.

- *Than, then.* The conjunction *than* connects the two parts of a comparison. The word *then* usually refers to time.

> He is taller than I am.
>
> We should have left then.

- *They're, their, there. They're* is a contraction of "they are." *Their* is a possessive pronoun. *There* usually shows location.

> They're on the roof.
>
> Their house is on the corner.
>
> There they are.

- *Who, whom. Who* is a subject; *whom* is an object. If you can replace *who* with *he* or *she*, you are using *who* correctly. If you can replace *whom* with *him* or *her*, you are using *whom* correctly. (You may have to revise the sentence temporarily to check.)

> Who said we wanted to go? (You can replace **who** with **he** or **she**.)
>
> To whom does Raquel speak? (You can replace **whom** with **him** or **her**. **Raquel speaks to her**.)

Understand It

1. On another sheet of paper, rewrite this paragraph, correcting the errors.

> I felt badly that he lost the race. Then again, its true that their wasn't much time. To train good for that race, you need more then just ability. You also need a good coach and the right diet. Whom was going to make sure he was laying down doing his push-ups?

Apply It

2. On a separate sheet of paper, write a paragraph about your favorite music. Use at least six examples of easily confused words.

Lesson 59 Spelling

When you're editing, it is important to check that you've spelled all the words correctly. Some words in English are spelled the way they sound. The words *step* and *tiger* are examples. Many English words, though, are not spelled the way they sound. The words *enough* and *written* are examples. Spelling matters, because incorrect spellings can cause your reader to miss your points.

Define It

Spelling has rules, although these rules don't apply to every English word. Here are some of the most common ways to improve your everyday spelling.

To begin spelling a word you're not sure about, sound it out by syllables. If you sound out *popularity*, for instance, you'll probably spell it correctly: *pop-u-lar-i-ty.*

More About Spelling Another way to improve your spelling is to train yourself not to assume that you know how to spell every word. Good writers rely on their dictionary or a computer spelling checker. Looking up a word can also help you remember its spelling.

Understand It

Here are some of the tricks for spelling troublesome words.

■ *Use -i before -e except after -c, or when -e and -i together sound like -a, as in* neighbor *and* weigh. Examples include *achieve, field,* and *sieve;* and *ceiling* and *deceive.*

■ *Watch out for silent letters.* Many of these words have to be memorized. Examples include *lamb, knife, sword,* and *psychology.*

■ *Watch out for homonyms.* Homonyms are words that sound alike but are spelled differently. Examples include *meat, meet, mete; sight, cite, site; peace, piece;* and *capital, capitol.*

■ *Know the difference between single words and two-word phrases that sound the same.* Examples include *everyday* (meaning "ordinary") and *every day* (meaning "each day"); *maybe* (meaning "perhaps") and *may be* (meaning "it could happen"); and *already* (meaning "previously") and *all ready* (meaning "prepared").

■ *If you use pronunciation as an aid to spelling, don't forget to include the final -ed.* In speech, the *-ed,* as in *used,* can get lost if you don't clearly hear it in speech. Examples include *ask* and *asked* and *ice* and *iced.*

■ *Watch for the difference between singular nouns that end in -nce and plural nouns that end in -nts.* Examples include *assistance* and *assistants; patience* and *patients;* and *instance* and *instants.*

▶ Work with a partner to find the spelling errors in the following sentences. Rewrite the sentences and correct the misspellings. If you have questions, look up the word in a dictionary.

1. If there going to go, they shud remember that there use to be no body there to give directions.

_____

2. Your peace of pizza has no meet on it.

_____

3. They get their regular, every day exercize by going to the field, the sight of the national champeunships.

_____

4. There is no reeson to sit staring at the cieling, hopeing that you're going to make the team.

_____

5. It maybe that they no what they're doing, but I want to give them assistants.

_____

6. In the passed, you new what you where suposed to do.

_____

Apply It

7. Review some writing you have done recently. Identify five words you often misspell. On the lines below, spell them correctly, then use each word in a sentence.

_____

_____

_____

_____

Lesson 60   Spelling Suffixes

■ ■

Adding a suffix to a word can change its part of speech, its tense, or its number. Suffixes allow writers to change the meaning of a word slightly or to form a new word.

Define It

Suffixes are syllables or groups of syllables that are added to the ends of words. Examples include *-ful*, as in *playful*; *-ed*, as in *joked*; *-ing*, as in *coming*; and *-th*, as in *seventh*.

Understand It

In all the examples above, some change is made either to the word or to the suffix when the suffix is added. Here are some rules you can use to help you improve your spelling of suffixes.

■ *When a word ends with a silent -e and the suffix begins with a vowel or -y, drop the -e.* Examples include *joke, joker; scare, scary;* and *tame, tamest.*

■ *When a verb ends with -ie, change the -ie to -y before you add -ing.* Examples include *lie, lying* and *tie, tying.*

■ *When a verb in the present tense ends with -y, change the -y to -ied to form the past tense.* Examples include *cry, cried* and *study, studied.*

■ *When you add -ness or -ly to a word, do not change the spelling of the word unless the word ends with -y.* Examples include *late, lateness; friend, friendly;* and *happy, happily.*

■ *When a one-syllable word ends with a single vowel and a single consonant and the suffix begins with a vowel, double the final consonant.* Examples include *bag, bagged* and *skip, skipped.*

1. Work with a partner to correct the spelling in the following paragraph.

> When Joe droped the ball, his freind was lieing on the ground. That's when the runer ran intoo Joe. Latter, Joe recoverred, and the runer tryed to help him stand up.

_____

_____

_____

Apply It

2. Work with a partner to review the spelling rules above. Then in the margin next to each one, add another example that illustrates the rule.

Lesson 61 Spelling Plurals

To pluralize most nouns, you simply add an -s. You would find it easy to pluralize *dog* in this way. Sometimes, however, plurals follow different rules. For example, you pluralize *goose* by changing the word to *geese*.

Define It

The **plural** form of a word shows that there is more than one of something.

Understand It

Here are some rules for spelling plurals.

- In most cases, you add -s to a noun that ends with a consonant. Examples include: *book, books* and *dog, dogs.*

  For nouns that end in -o *preceded by a vowel, add* -s. Examples include *radio, radios* and *zoo, zoos.* (Exception: *For some nouns that end in* -o, *add* -es. Examples include *tomato, tomatoes* and *hero, heroes.*)

  For nouns that end in -ff, *add* -s. Examples include *sheriff, sheriffs* and *bluff, bluffs.*

- You add -es in other cases.

  For singular nouns that end with -s, -c, -ch, -sh, -x, *or* -z, *add* -es. Examples include *business, businesses; box, boxes; catch, catches;* and *dash, dashes.*

  For nouns that end in a consonant and -y, *change the* -y *to* -i. Examples include *thirty, thirties* and *fly, flies.*

 More About Plurals For proper nouns that end in -y, add only -s. Here is an example: the *Gradys* (plural for the *Grady* family).

  For nouns that end in -f *or* -fe, *change the* -f *or* -fe *to* -v *and add* -es. Examples include *half, halves* and *knife, knives.* (Exception: *Some words don't follow this rule.* Examples include *spoof, spoofs* and *belief, beliefs.*)

▶ In the following sentences, correct the spelling errors and write the corrected sentence on the lines below. If you aren't sure of a spelling, look it up in the dictionary.

1. His deeply held beliefes mean that he never cheats businesss.

2. There are two Russ on the busses that will take us to the rodeoes.

_____

_____

3. Usually, he is the first to go to the mailboxs.

_____

_____

4. The three boyes had all the radioes in their cars, ready to take to partys.

_____

_____

Apply It

5. On the lines below, write a paragraph that describes a trip you have taken to a store. Be sure to mention several items that you bought.

_____

_____

_____

_____

_____

_____

_____

1. Revise this report, using editing marks. As you read the report, look for spelling errors, as well as errors in coherence and unity.

Have you ever had an ice cream headache? You might have thought it was only in you're head. My brother got one, but I told him he just didn't like the kind of ice cream he was eating. Sceintists who have been studing the ice cream headache say its real.

These sceintists found that about 30 percent of people get ice cream headachs. These people eat a spoonful of ice cream and feel a stabing pane in they're face or head. It's a pain that can last for five minuts.

The sceintists who studyied these headaches found the anser to the puzle. They like ice cream, to. they discoverd that when the ice cream hitts the bak of the mouth, it hits the nerves their and cuases the headachs. If you want to keep from geting ice cream headaches, just don't gulp ice ceram so its hiting the back of yor mouth.

2. On a separate sheet of paper, revise a paper you have written. As you find errors, or better ways to write things, use editing marks to note the changes. When you have finished, rewrite the paper. Compare your original with your revision. What changes did you make?

UNIT 3   Editor's Checklist

Editing your work is an important step in the writing process. After you have completed your first draft, make sure that your work is clear and that it says what you want to say.

Use this checklist to help you assess your writing for style, organization, and spelling errors.

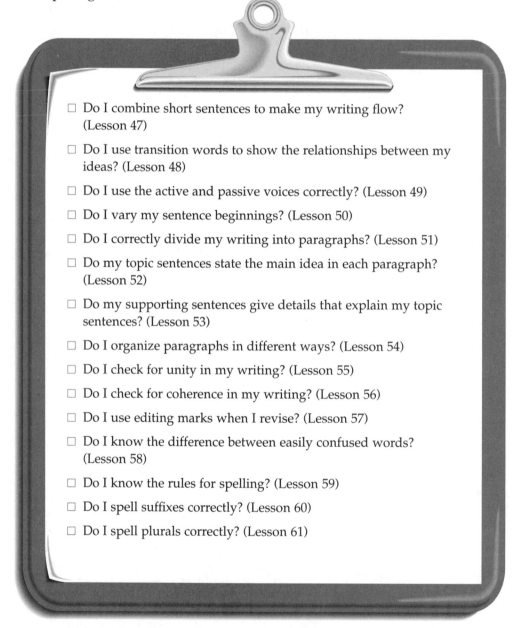

□ Do I combine short sentences to make my writing flow? (Lesson 47)

□ Do I use transition words to show the relationships between my ideas? (Lesson 48)

□ Do I use the active and passive voices correctly? (Lesson 49)

□ Do I vary my sentence beginnings? (Lesson 50)

□ Do I correctly divide my writing into paragraphs? (Lesson 51)

□ Do my topic sentences state the main idea in each paragraph? (Lesson 52)

□ Do my supporting sentences give details that explain my topic sentences? (Lesson 53)

□ Do I organize paragraphs in different ways? (Lesson 54)

□ Do I check for unity in my writing? (Lesson 55)

□ Do I check for coherence in my writing? (Lesson 56)

□ Do I use editing marks when I revise? (Lesson 57)

□ Do I know the difference between easily confused words? (Lesson 58)

□ Do I know the rules for spelling? (Lesson 59)

□ Do I spell suffixes correctly? (Lesson 60)

□ Do I spell plurals correctly? (Lesson 61)

UNIT 3 What Have You Learned?

True or False   In the blanks, write *T* for true or *F* for false. Then correct the errors.

1. _____ *The play was seen by him.* That sentence is an example of the active voice.

_____

2. _____ *I like to fish; as a result, I have four fishing rods.* In that sentence, *I* is a transition word.

_____

3. _____ The topic sentence should appear at the end of the paragraph.

_____

4. _____ *Bob, lie down now.* In that sentence, *lie* is correct.

_____

5. _____ *Its not a sunny day.* There are no errors in that sentence.

_____

Correct the Errors   In each of the following sentences, circle the word that is misused or misspelled and write it correctly in the space. If the sentence has no errors, write *none*.

6. _____ He needed five boxes for their supplies and six brushes for painting.

7. _____ The tomatos in their salads tasted funny to Jimmy and Devon.

8. _____ The teacher said, "Lyeing about what you did will only make things worse."

9. _____ He did really good on his test.

10. _____ Geri didn't receive the package.

The Writing Process

The writing process   What happens when a writer turns words into a story or an essay? He or she follows a set of steps, from start to finish. These steps make up the writing process. If you follow the same steps, you can make the process work for you.

What is a process?   A process is a series of steps that lead to a goal. Each step brings the process closer to the goal. Suppose you wanted to grow a pepper plant in a pot. Growing a plant is a process. You choose seeds, plant them, water the plants, and pull weeds. Each step gets you closer to your goal, and finally you pick the peppers.

What is the writing process?   There are five main steps in the writing process. They are prewriting, drafting, revising, proofreading, and publishing. This chart shows them. You won't always follow them in order, and you may move back and forth between stages.

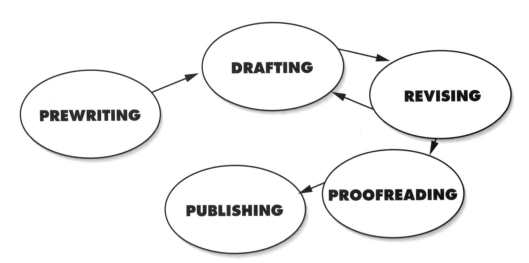

Prewriting   In prewriting, you decide what to write. This step is like deciding what seeds to grow. You explore your idea. You think about it and gather information about it. You organize your ideas. You think about the people you will be writing for. You decide what they need to know and how you want to tell it to them.

Drafting   In drafting, you put your ideas into words. You shape your words into sentences. You build your sentences into paragraphs. As you draft, you do not have to worry about parts that are not quite right. You will fix them in the next stage.

Revising   In revising, you improve your draft. You look for weak spots, such as a word or a sentence that is not quite right. You make changes, or revisions, to strengthen those spots. Notice that the arrows in the drafting and revising sections can lead you back and forth. This part of the process is like watering and weeding in the growing process.

Proofreading   When you are satisfied with your revised work, you turn to proofreading. This stage is sometimes called editing. In this step, you check for and correct any errors you may have made in grammar, usage, and mechanics, including spelling.

Publishing   Finally, in the publishing stage, you make a final copy of your work and publish it or share it with an audience.

Modes of Writing

Persuasive Writing

Persuasive writing expresses an opinion. Effective persuasive writing shows why opinions, beliefs, or ideas are reasonable.

When you write to persuade, follow these guidelines: State your opinion on an issue. Use facts, examples, and reasons to support that opinion. Present your argument logically. Urge your readers to think differently or take an action. End on a positive note.

As you edit your persuasive writing, check these points: Are my reasons presented convincingly? Do they support my position? Is my organization clear and consistent?

Narrative Writing

Narrative writing tells a story. Effective narrative writing makes the reader feel like he or she is part of the story. You might use narrative writing to tell about an experience or to tell a story.

When you write a narrative, follow these guidelines: Build your story around a plot or a series of events. Describe your characters and the scene clearly and vividly.

As you edit your narrative writing, check these points: Is my writing well-organized? Does it have a clear order of events with a beginning, a middle, and an end? Do my ideas flow smoothly?

Expository Writing

Expository writing explains or informs. Effective expository writing clearly explains an idea. You might use expository writing to summarize a book or article or to explain how to do something.

When you write to explain, follow these guidelines: Use examples and facts that support your ideas. Present your ideas in a clear, organized way. Add details to make your explanation clear.

As you edit your expository writing, check these points: Does my essay explain my topic? Do I present the information clearly and logically? Does each paragraph have a well-developed idea that includes details, examples, or reasons to support my main point?

Descriptive Writing

Descriptive writing paints a picture in words. Effective descriptive writing lets the reader experience what you're describing.

When you write to describe, follow these guidelines: Close your eyes and form a picture of your topic. Think of details that will make the scene come alive for your reader. Use vivid words.

As you edit your descriptive writing, check these points: Does my writing clearly describe something or someone? Is my organization logical? Do I use rich language and exciting details?

A Guide for Writers: Terms to Know

active voice In the active voice, the subject performs the action. Example: *Julie sawed the log. Julie*, the subject, performed the action. **p. 91**

adjective An adjective modifies a noun or pronoun. Example: *What a great catch.* The adjective *great* modifies the noun *catch*. **p. 35**

adverb An adverb modifies a verb, an adjective, or another adverb. Example: *Sandra danced gracefully.* The adverb *gracefully* modifies the verb *danced*. **p. 36**

antecedent The antecedent of a pronoun is the word to which the pronoun refers. Example: *Posey looked at her schedule. Posey* is the antecedent of the pronoun *her.* **pp. 60–61**

apostrophe An apostrophe is often used with contractions and possessives. Example: *Nora's mother said she shouldn't do that.* The apostrophe in *Nora's* shows possession and the apostrophe in *shouldn't* shows that the word is a contraction. **pp. 74–75**

capitalization Capitalization, or using an upper-case letter at the start of a word, marks the beginning of a sentence and shows proper nouns and proper adjectives. Example: *He traveled to Italy.* **pp. 66–67**

cause and effect You can organize a paragraph by cause and effect by showing how one event caused another. **p. 101**

chronological order You can organize a paragraph in chronological order, or time order, by presenting events in the order in which they happened. **p. 100**

classification You can use classification in a paragraph by creating categories for your supporting details. **p. 101**

clear pronoun reference Use clear antecedents when you use pronouns. Example of unclear reference: *He took it to heart.* Clear reference: *Dave took my advice to heart.* **p. 63**

coherence When you revise for coherence, make sure that your ideas are arranged in a logical order. Also check that your ideas flow smoothly from one idea to the next. **p. 105**

colon Use a colon to direct attention to what is to follow. Example: *We have decided: Mary will represent our class on the team.* **p. 73**

combining sentences When you combine sentences, put several short sentences together so the new sentence contains related ideas. **pp. 88–89**

comma Use a comma to separate words, phrases, or clauses; to group parts of a sentence; or to show when to pause in reading. Example: *If you want to visit, please let us know.* **pp. 70–71**

comma fault A comma fault occurs when a comma connects two sentences that don't belong together. Example: *Meet us at the park, we won't be late.* Correct: *Meet us at the park. We won't be late.* **p. 21**

common noun A common noun names any person, place, thing, or idea. Example: *We played basketball. Basketball* is a common noun. **p. 31**

comparative degree The comparative degree in adjectives and adverbs compares two things. Example: *Ned eats faster than Julie. Faster* shows the comparative degree. **p. 56**

compare When you compare, you show how items are alike. **p. 101**

complete predicate The complete predicate includes the verb and all the words that give more information about the verb. Example: *The two friends laughed away their worries.* The complete predicate is *laughed away their worries.* **p. 9**

complete subject The complete subject includes the subject and all the words that describe or give more information about the simple subject. Example: *The singer Graciela performed first.* The complete subject is *The singer Graciela.* **p. 9**

complex sentence A complex sentence has an independent clause and one or more dependent clauses. Example: *While we were waiting, the players took the field.* **p. 12**

compound noun Compound nouns are made up of two or more words that act as one noun. Example: *Eat that hot dog. Hot dog* is a compound noun. **p. 31**

compound predicate A compound predicate has more than one simple predicate. Example: *Devon dribbled and shot. Dribbled and shot* is the compound predicate. **p. 10**

compound sentence A compound sentence has two or more independent clauses. Example: *We arrived, and the music was playing.* **p. 11**

compound subject A compound subject has more than one subject. Example: *Dale and Michael shared the pizza. Dale and Michael* is the compound subject. **p. 10**

conjunction A conjunction joins words, phrases, and clauses. Example: *Maeve and I danced.* The word *and* connects *Maeve* and *I.* **p. 40**

contrast When you contrast, you show how items are different. **p. 101**

coordinating conjunction A coordinating conjunction links words, clauses, and phrases that have the same grammatical structure. Example: *We swam, but they read. But* is a coordinating conjunction. **p. 40**

dangling modifier A dangling modifier is a phrase, usually at the beginning of a sentence, that does not appear to be connected to anything in the sentence. Example: *Not being able to read, the teacher helped him.* Correct: *The teacher helped him because he was unable to read.* **p. 18**

dash A dash shows a sharp turn in the thought of a sentence or encloses explanations or examples. Example: *Our teacher—our English teacher—is sitting at that table.* **p. 78**

declarative sentence A declarative sentence makes a statement. Example: *My dog sits.* **p. 3**

dependent clause A dependent clause contains a subject and predicate, but it cannot stand alone as a complete sentence. Example: *If you want to come in, go to the side door. If you want to come in* is a dependent clause. **p. 12**

direct object The direct object of the verb is a word or group of words that receives the action of the verb. Example: *We remember our friends. Our friends* is the direct object. **p. 52**

editing marks Writers and editors use editing marks to show where they want to revise their writing. **p. 107**

example An example can clarify a point or illustrate a paragraph's main idea. **p. 99**

exclamation point An exclamation point ends an exclamatory sentence, a forceful imperative sentence, and a strong interjection. Example: *Stop that train!* **p. 5, 6, 69**

exclamatory sentence An exclamatory sentence expresses strong feeling or emotion. Example: *I can't believe you won!* **p. 6**

fact A fact is a statement you can prove. Facts are often used to support or explain a topic sentence. **p. 98**

future tense The future tense of a verb shows that an action has not yet happened. Example: *We will go to the movies tomorrow.* **p. 47**

hyphen A hyphen can divide words that are too long to fit on a line or join two or more words to make a single adjective or a compound word. Example: *The chocolate-covered cherries are delicious.* **p. 80**

imperative sentence An imperative sentence makes a request or gives a command. Example: *Meet me at the gym in an hour.* **p. 5**

indefinite pronoun Indefinite pronouns refer to no specific person, place, thing, or idea. Example: *Everyone knows the secret. Everyone* is an indefinite pronoun. **p. 34**

independent clause An independent clause is a group of words that has a subject and a predicate and can stand alone as a complete sentence. Example: *My friends danced.* **p. 10**

indirect object The indirect object of the verb is often used with verbs of telling, asking, and receiving. It answers the questions *to what?* or *to whom?* Example: *We gave Bob the menu. Bob* is the indirect object. **p. 52**

interjection An interjection is a word or expression that shows surprise or strong feeling. Example: *Well! I guess you don't need my help. Well!* is an interjection. **p. 42**

interrogative sentence An interrogative sentence asks a question and ends with a question mark. Example: *Did you buy the milk?* **p. 4**

irregular verbs An irregular verb does not follow a predictable pattern when it changes tense. Example: *We build a sand castle today. We built a sand castle yesterday. Build* is an irregular verb. **pp. 48–49**

mechanics Mechanics is the term for punctuation marks, capitalization, and italics. **p. 65**

misplaced modifier A misplaced modifier is a modifier that is in the wrong position. Example: *The baker kneaded the dough wearing the apron.* Correct: *The baker wearing the apron kneaded the dough.* **p. 16**

modifier A modifier is a word or group of words that describes other words. Example: *Tired and cold, we arrived at the cabin. Tired and cold* are modifiers that describe *we.* **p. 16**

noun A noun names a person, place, thing, or idea. Example: *The wolf howled. Wolf* is a noun. **p. 31**

numbers Numbers of less than one hundred and numbers that are rounded to hundreds are usually spelled out. They are also spelled out if they begin a sentence. Example: *Two hundred students joined the 354 who were already at the high school.* **p. 82**

object pronoun An object pronoun acts as the object of a verb. Example: *Hong told her to turn left. Her* is the object of the verb *told.* **p. 54**

order of importance You can organize a paragraph by the order of importance of the ideas. **pp. 100–101**

organizing paragraphs When you organize paragraphs, you decide how you will structure your paragraphs. **p. 100**

paragraph A paragraph is a group of sentences that develops an idea or topic. **p. 96**

parallelism Parallelism in writing is a repetition of grammatical forms. Example: *He played soccer, took a shower, and ate lunch.* The phrases *played soccer, took a shower,* and *ate lunch* are parallel in form. **pp. 24–25**

parentheses Parentheses give a reader additional information, but minimize its importance. Example: *Ted (Alice's boyfriend) is on the bench.* **p. 78**

parts of speech The parts of speech are the eight groups into which words can be classified: nouns, verbs, pronouns, adjectives, adverbs, prepositions, conjunctions, and interjections. **p. 30**

passive voice In the passive voice, the subject of the sentence does not perform the action of the sentence. Example: *The ceiling was painted by him.* **p. 91**

past participle This verb form is created by adding the words *have, has,* or *had* before the past tense verb. Example: *We have waited four months for that letter.* **p. 47**

past tense The past tense of a verb signals that the action has already happened. Example: *We laid in the sun.* **p. 46**

period A period is used to end a declarative sentence or a mild imperative sentence. In addition, periods are used with initials in a person's name and to show that a word has been abbreviated. Example: *Harry ate the pie.* **p. 3, 5, 68**

personal pronoun Personal pronouns refer to specific people or things. Example: *He bowed to the queen. He* is a personal pronoun. **p. 33**

phrase A phrase is a group of words that does not have a subject and a predicate and cannot stand alone. Example: *We will leave after dinner. After dinner* is a phrase. **p. 15**

plural The plural form of the word shows that there is more than one of something. Spelling rules for plurals are on **p. 113**.

positive degree The positive degree in adverbs and adjectives describes only one thing. Example: *Maura is hungry.* **p. 56**

possessive pronoun A possessive pronoun shows ownership. Example: *There is his notebook. His* is a possessive pronoun. **pp. 33–34**

predicate The predicate is the verb or verb phrase that tells what the subject is doing. Example: *Robert might have won the trophy.* The predicate is *might have won the trophy.* **p. 9**

preposition A preposition shows the relationship between a noun or pronoun and another word in a sentence. Example: *Gerald walked beside the referee. Beside* is a preposition that shows where Gerald is in relation to the referee. **pp. 38–39**

present participle The present participle is a form of the present tense in which *-ing* is added to the present tense verb. It is used with a helping verb such as *is* or *are.* Example: *We are helping bring in the harvest. Helping* is the present participle form of the verb *help.* **p. 46**

present tense The present tense of a verb shows that something is happening now. Example: *Marta walks toward the door.* **p. 46**

pronoun A pronoun is a word that takes the place of a noun. Example: *He dropped it. He* and *it* are pronouns. **pp. 33–34**

proper adjective Proper adjectives are formed from proper nouns and begin with a capital letter. Example: *Our Swedish friend taught me to dance. Swedish* is a proper adjective. **p. 35**

proper noun A proper noun names a particular person, place, thing, or idea. Proper nouns begin with a capital letter. Example: *Kate left for Miami on Friday. Kate, Miami,* and *Friday* are proper nouns. **p. 31**

question mark A question mark ends an interrogative sentence. Example: *Did you see the concert?* **p. 4, 69**

quotation marks Quotation marks go around the actual words someone has spoken or written. Example: *"Come back,"* LeShawn called. **pp. 76–77**

reason Reasons are statements that explain or give more information to show that a topic sentence is correct. **p. 99**

regular verb A regular verb changes its form in a predictable way, depending on its subject's person and number. Example: *You reach the finish line. You reached the finish line. Reach* is a regular verb. **pp. 46–47**

run-on sentence A run-on sentence strings together two or more sentences without using a linking word or punctuation to connect them. Example: *We went to the store we left before lunch.* Correct: *We went to the store; we left before lunch.* **p. 20**

semicolon A semicolon groups similar grammatical forms within a sentence. In addition, a semicolon groups items in a list that has commas within the items. Example: *We ate grapes; they ate raspberries.* **p. 72**

sentence A sentence is a unit of thought that ends with a period, a question mark, or an exclamation point. **p. 1**

sentence fragment A sentence fragment is a phrase that lacks either a subject or a predicate. Example: *Hurt his knee.* Correct: *Charlie hurt his knee.* **p. 19**

simple predicate A simple predicate is the verb in a sentence. Example: *The two friends laughed away their worries. Laughed* is the simple predicate. **p. 9**

simple sentence A simple sentence has one independent clause. Example: *We ate the green beans.* **p. 10**

simple subject The simple subject is the most important word in the complete subject. Example: *The talented singer Graciela performed first.* The simple subject is *Graciela.* **p. 9**

spatial order You can organize a paragraph in spatial order by describing how something appears in space. **p. 100**

spelling Spelling rules are on **pp. 110–113**.

story Supporting sentences can tell a story and create a picture in the reader's mind. **p. 98**

subject The subject of a sentence is what or whom the sentence is about. Subjects can be nouns or pronouns. Example: *James ran down the hill*. The subject is *James*. **p. 9**

subject pronoun A subject pronoun acts as the subject of a sentence. Example: *We left the store. We* is the subject of the sentence. **p. 54**

subject-verb agreement Subjects and verbs agree when both are either singular or plural. Example: *They fly at night*. Both *they* and *fly* are plural. **pp. 57–58**

subordinating conjunction A subordinating conjunction joins a dependent clause to an independent clause. Example: *Before Ella arrived, we cleaned the room. Before* is a coordinating conjunction. **p. 40**

suffix A suffix is a syllable or group of syllables added to the ends of a word. **p. 112**

superlative degree The superlative degree in adjectives and adverbs compares more than two things. Example: *She is the nicest of the three sisters. Nicest* shows the superlative degree. **p. 56**

supporting sentence A supporting sentence gives details that explain a topic sentence. **pp. 98–99**

tense A verb's tense shows the time of the action or the state of being that is described. The three basic tenses are past, present, and future.

Example: *Charlene made the cake. Made* is the past tense of make. **p. 45**

titles Titles for books, articles, and movies are sometimes written in quotes and sometimes written in italics or underlined. **p. 81**

topic sentence The main idea of a paragraph—the paragraph's purpose—is often expressed in a topic sentence. **p. 97**

transition words A transition word shows the relationship between ideas in sentences and ideas in paragraphs. Example: *We walked too much; as a result, our legs were sore. As a result* is a group of transition words. **p. 90**

unity A paragraph has unity if all of its supporting sentences are directly related to its topic sentence. **p. 104**

varying sentences When you vary sentences, you use different openings and lengths of sentences. **p. 87**

verb A verb is the part of speech that shows action or a state of being. Example: *We ran for the bus. Ran* is a verb. **p. 32**

verb tense consistency Verb tense consistency means being sure that your verbs show the correct time relationship to one another. Example: *We slept while the workers finish.* Correct: *We slept while the workers finished.* **p. 50**

wordiness Wordiness is using more words than are necessary to say what you want to say. Example: *During the same time that we were skating, Bob was sleeping.* Correct: *While we were skating, Bob was sleeping.* **pp. 22–23**